IELTS Speaking on the GO

Bipin Patel

ISBN - 0000000

First Edition : 2012

Published by : Mr. Bipin Patel
mahi educational services
16, Marutinandan-2 Patan Road, Unjha - 384 170
Dist. : Mehsana
Gujarat, India
Ph. : +91 8866863352
E-mail : bipin.ielts@gmail.com
: mahi13.edu@gmail.com

Distributed by : M.K.Book Distributors
1, Tulsi Complex,2 Azad Society,
Ambawadi, Ahmedabad - 380 015
Ph. : 079 - 26763012/22
E-mail : mkbooksd@gmail.com
: mkbook@vsnl.net
Website : www.mkbooksd.com

CONTENTS

Acknowledgment

Million thanks to Mr. Hiren Bhatt for having been with me since the beginning. Had his continuous support not been there, perhaps this book would never have taken the material shape. His assistance in writing, extensive proofreading, effective suggestions and many more have played a great role in my venture.

I really thank Mr. Indrubhai and Mohanbhai for showing keen interest in this book and helping me out whenever I felt the need.

I here want to thank each and everybody of my support team, particularly Chirag Patel, Urvesh Patel and all those who readily accepted my proposal of facing a camera in an impromptu manner.

Author's Corner

When my wife, Vaishali once told me to do my bit in this project. I readily accepted it. I almost instantly suggested the title also.

It was a fascinating project. Very interesting, very challenging. It amounted to making research, deep and wide: to create, recreate and reproduce; and ultimately to edit it all according to the dictates of the basic requirements of IELTS speaking.

It was a formidabli task but an overwhelming spirit to give something to the students helped me to overcome the challenge and made the task an interesting one. But all fascinating things are stupendous! I plunged deep down into it immediately, and when surfaced, the stipulated time was over.

I believe I would have produced this book quite earlier so I sincerely regret the delay – especially to Vaishali.

The aim of the book is not to feed students with readymade ideas and sentences. Google can do that well. The aim is skill building. In my knowledge, this is the only book which makes students familiar with extensive practice of fluency and pronunciation, two most important assessment criteria of IELTS speaking. Students always tend to overlook them. List of cohesive devises given in this book is unique one. If learnt in an assimilative manner, they will help any learner of English make sentences on his own. The list of speaking tips is the result of wide experience of teaching students for over 10 years.

This book will serve to be an important tool to those who do not find time for coaching (especially the students of the general module). It will be a handy material for them. You can understand what fluency and pronunciations are and even how to answer questions in part 1 and 3. This book will make it possible while lying on the bed and plugging your ears with earphones, while driving a car, in the leisure time in an office. If I am not exaggerating, I can say that this book will be a keep-in-the-pocket kind of teacher for all. All these efforts will be well rewarded if all the readers improve their speaking skill and eventually contribute at least one and half bands to their existing level, though later is not the aim of the book. The basic aim of the book is to make students make sentences on their own and speak them with acceptable pronunciation and reasonably impressive fluency.

Bipin patel.

Recognition

As far as I know this is the only book in the history of IELTS which gives an extensive practice in fluency and pronunciation. I can understand the pains and pangs of recording so many interviews in such an excellent manner. It must have taken many days of recording, deleting, adding, editing and finalizing. Being a writer and a tutor of English language, I can say that it is not less than making a movie. This book is Bipin's sincere attempt to give something to IELTS aspirants. Though he terms it 'a small attempt', I would like to say this is a great breakthrough in the literature of IELTS. I wish this book could have come up some years ago.

This book would certainly help all but it will prove to be a great boon to those coming from non-English medium background. It effectively cracks the myths surrounding speaking module.

Hiren Bhatt. (Writer and trainer)

Three things to bear in mind to enjoy this book....

(1)

It appears silly to refer to both the genders all the time when required so I have referred to masculine gender only. This should not be taken as a gender bias but rather a convenience. To write "he/she", "him/her" and "his/her" is really boring so all the readers are kindly expected not to take it amiss and understand the gender the reader himself or herself is.

(2)

You will find a lot of difference between the language used from the interview no.1 to 25 and from interview no. 26 to 50. This is deliberately done to serve two purposes. In the first segment (from 1 to 25) the choice of words, quality of sentence construction and the use of cohesive devises are of highly extra ordinary level. The students who already have a good level of language especially the students who have been educated in English medium schools will find them really interesting and helpful. The second segment (from 26 to 50) is written keeping in mind the students who are good at English but do not have exceptionally good command of English language. The students who have been educated in non English medium schools will find them most interesting. The kind of words, cohesive devises and sentence construction used in those interviews will be of a great help to them. Remember, these interviews are not to feed you with the ideas. Plenty of ideas can be availed from many sources. Look at the words. Look at the sentence constructions. Look at the cohesive devises.

(3)

Somewhere you will find that answers are written keeping the academic module in mind and somewhere you will find that answers are written keeping the general module in mind. Answers differ only in speaking part 1since all the question are individualized. Part 2 and 3 are general in nature. Speaking module, assessment criteria and evaluation process are completely same. So you are requested to take the full advantage of this book irrespective of the module you have opted for.

10 important facts to develop speaking skills....

A newly born baby cultivates speaking ability long before he learns how to read and write.

Many students are seen reading the answers in the book before they speak them. It is linguistically proven that if a person is to develop his speaking skills, he should listen to that language as much as he can. Wide exposure to language will make the person a good communicator. Extensive reading will undoubtedly feed the person with many ideas but speaking is altogether a different area of language. Watching English movies, listening to news on the television are some of the ways to cultivate good speaking skills because we get a chance to know what fluency and pronunciation is all about.

Good writers are not necessarily good speakers.

To know English is totally different from to speak it well. Many students are under the impression that they will be able to speak well in examination because they score six or seven bands in writing module. It is a myth which gets demystified in the exam. Until and unless you practice extensively, you will not be able to achieve good command. Writing gives you enough time to express your ideas while in speaking module, thinking and speaking go on simultaneously which leaves little possibility of making corrections and thinking of good sentence patterns. To get rid of flaws in the pronunciation, one must speak more and more.

Speaking skills can be improved by speaking only.

Speaking and writing are popularly known as productive skills. Your level of language is completely exposed in both the modules. There is nothing like wonders or miracles in the speaking module. A candidate has to speak English as much as he can. Make English not a subject but a habit. Prefer English to converse with your friends. Make such company. Don't limit your speaking practice to classroom only. Keep in the mind that your tutor is there to guide you and correct your errors; he can not speak on behalf of you. Never have the fear of being laughed at by others. Our aim is to develop our speaking skills and not to please others.

Cramming sentences is the worst idea to score well in speaking module.

Remember well, IELTS examiners are so well trained that they easily can evaluate your ability to speak English spontaneously. Speaking two to three good sentences can never convince your examiner of your being able to speak well if the rest of the interview is filled with errors and flaws. Instead of copying the sentences made by others, you make your own. Remember, it is better to make a faulty sentence on your own than to copy an accurate sentence. Never mug up the answers as it will make you appear diffident in examination hall. A candidate will anyhow try to accommodate his pre prepared sentences to the given topic which is easily noticed by an examiner and it will mar the charm and basic purpose of the speaking examination. Be original.

Only grammar is not important, you are also observed for your ability to speak English

clearly and in an understandable accent.

Very honestly speaking, even in coaching centers less emphasis is laid upon these two important aspects of speaking. Candidate is not expected to have British or American accent to score well but he should at least be able to pronounce the basic words clearly and correctly. This doesn't require the special training in phonetics (science of pronunciation). However wide exposure to listening will make one aware of the right pronunciation. Remember, we speak what we hear.

I read, I forget.
I listen, I remember.
I speak, I understand.

This is a universally proven truth. The tragedy with most of the IELTS candidates is that they always strive to improve their speaking skills by reading the answers which is very poor and not so yielding way of developing speaking skills.
The best way is....... Read less. Listen more. Speak most.

Students who have been educated in English medium schools are always good scorers in IELTS is a big myth and needs to be busted.

Students with English background do certainly have good stock of words and have got that environment which quite naturally makes them better speakers. But it doesn't mean that students educated in their mother tongue can't do so. As per the education psychology, students good at mother tongue take very less time in learning other languages. Here I will not fail to mention that great speakers of English like Swami Vivekananda, Gandhi, and Aurbindo were educated in their mother tongue only.

Confidence is nothing but a positive mindset which is the result of being well prepared.

"You must not be stressed while facing the interview and your face must reflect confidence. " Every student preparing for IELTS must have heard this sentence from their tutors in coaching centers. But what is this confidence? Where is it available? How much does it cost? There is no need to focus more on this factor. If you are mentally well prepared to face the speaking interview and have ability to make sentences on your own on any given topic, your face will exude confidence without being unduly conscious of that.

Never pay any heed to what other unauthorized people say about this important module.

"I got less score because the examiner seemed to have disagreed to what I said " the examiner seemed to have been exhausted after conducting so many interviews so I was not given proper justice"
"In the evening, speaking interviews are conducted in a haste so there is a chance of getting a good score"
"The examiners in British council are stingy and in IDP they are generous "

"Examiners tend to be lenient if candidates happen to belong to their place or they happen to know them"

These are some of the most common sentences heard in IELTS student fraternity.
All these sentences are baseless. There is very objectively monitored and strict system of evaluating speaking interviews and perhaps that is the reason that they are audio recorded. The assessment criteria are too objective to leave any room for subjective perception. Never get misled by all these gossips and buzzes since all the examiners are extensively trained in the evaluation process. However candidate can always go for reassessment if he is not satisfied with his result.

Getting bad score at first attempt is not an indication that you do not know English well.
I have seen in my experience of teaching IELTS for more than ten years that even good English speakers end up scoring poorly. The reasons are many. Being over conscious due to expectations by peers and relatives sometimes make candidates stressed. Some candidates have never experienced this way of giving individualized examination. If the above mentioned are the reasons for your poor score, never hesitate to reappear as the previous failure will make you overcome your weakness. Here I express my fear that this should not be taken as an excuse to hide your weakness. Candidate himself is the best judge and that is needless to say.

ASSESSMENT CRITERIA OF SPEAKING MODULE

1. Fluency and coherence Fluency

Definition

Fluency means an ability to talk with normal levels of continuity with ease and reasonable speed. Speaking too fast should never be mistaken as fluency. Fast speech confuses listeners while slow speech bores them. You do not have to speak quickly but you have to speak smoothly. Keep your language flowing smoothly and confidently. The best measurement is the usual speed with which we talk in our daily conversation.

Steps to overcome the weakness...

The problem with fluency is that if we try to be fluent, grammatical accuracy is affected and if we stick to accuracy, fluency is affected. Initially never worry if you speak slowly. There is no point in achieving fluency at the cost of accuracy. But gradually the pace must increase. This can be easily achieved if you make English speaking a daily habit. Some silly ideas to do so are misusing toll free numbers. You can make calls to your telecom service provider and talk in English though there is no problem. Make calls to advertising companies and talk in English. Celebrate an English day in a week with your friends and speak only in English on that day. Fix a penalty for those who breach the condition. Extensive use of English in your daily life will make English a tongue friendly language.

Coherence

Definition

It is an ability to link all the ideas together effectively so the speech appear connected and logically consistent.

Steps to overcome the weakness...

Always sequence sentences in the order of information.

Mark the stages when you narrate, describe or argue.

Most importantly learn the use of connectors, pronouns, prepositions, conjunctions, phrase prepositions within and between the sentences.

The best way to do so is to refer to a good book of grammar and first know the correct uses of them and then apply them to your daily practice.

2. Lexical Resource

Definition

It is a range of candidate's vocabulary and appropriate use of them in the speech.
Using right words at the right time is more important than using very difficult words at the wrong time.

Steps to overcome the weakness....

Read English newspaper and magazines to get new words and find out their meanings. Try to learn the words contextually in order to avoid the ambiguity of meanings.

For example,
Look at the sentences below.
1. Rahul hates the subject of mathematics.
2. Akbar was deeply loved by his subject.
In the first sentence subject means something students have to study while in the second sentence it means the people of the kingdom.

Students will never understand the correct applications of the words if they do not learn them contextually. Merely knowing the meaning of the word will not help unless you know where and when to use it. "Where "stands for their applicability while "when" stands for their grammatical role.

Beginners can start with story books and fairy tales. Remember there is no shame in learning.

Candidates must develop the ability to fill the pauses or a vocabulary gap with other word and phrases without noticeable hesitations.

Develop a hunger in you to know more and more words. Learning new words require an irrepressible urge to know. Always look for the new words as if a drought victim looks for the food.

3. Grammatical range and accuracy

Definition

Accuracy refers to candidate's ability to make error free sentences.
Range refers to how appropriately the sentences are used. Apart from being grammatically correct, the sentences must be grammatically relevant too.

Steps to overcome the weakness

Learn the variety of simple, compound and complex sentences.
It is important to know the proper use of subordinate clauses.
A candidate must develop the ability to move parts of the sentences around for information focus and highlighting.

Accuracy is measured by the degree of acceptability of a given speech and its range is measured by the way errors affect the communication.

Beginners must be clear about the basic understanding of tenses, articles and active-passive constructions. Again there is no shame in learning. Go back to what we used to learn in our grammar sessions in 10th and 12th standards. Candidates can take the support of good grammar books.

4. Pronunciation

Definition

It is an ability to produce the speech in the comprehensible manner.
Accent must be neutral. Sounds must be clear. Words should be stressed for meaning and importance. Natural rhythm must be maintained. Syllables too must be maintained.
Candidate's speech should not cause strain to the examiner. Candidate's first language should not affect the way he speaks English language.
Always speak audibly.

Steps to overcome the weakness...

Listen more and more to standard English. Listening to foreign sports commentators, listening to English news channels, watching English movies are some of the ways to know how the native users of English pronounce words.
The best way is to make the ample use of the tape scripts of Listening tests in IELTS.
Just listen to them to know how the dialogues are spoken. You will know where to stress the word and how stressing different words alter the meaning of the whole sentence.
Below is an example of how the entire meaning changes just by locating and stressing the same word at different places in the sentences. Meanings are given in the bracket.

1. ONLY I hit him in the eye yesterday. (No one else did)
2. I ONLY hit him in the eye yesterday. (Did not slap him)
3. I hit ONLY him in the eye yesterday. (I did not hit others)
4. I hit him ONLY in the eye yesterday. (I did not hit outside the eye)
5. I hit him in ONLY the eye yesterday. (Not other organs)
6. I hit him in the ONLY eye yesterday. (He doesn't have another eye)
7. I hit him in the eye ONLY yesterday. (Not today)
8. I hit him in the eye yesterday ONLY. (Did not wait for today)

However there is no need to go through the whole science of phonetics. Little awareness will help the candidate.

LIST OF COHESIVE DEVISES

All the below listed expressions will be a great help to the Candidates to fill the gap between two sentences. They will reduce your hesitations and will make you more fluent. They will bring about variety in your answers and save you from being accused of being monotonous and repeating the same expressions. All these expressions can be used interchangeably but it is required to understand the context to make their uses more effective.

To express the agreement

I do agree with the idea that............

Question – Do you think heavy penalty to those who break traffic rules will decrease the offence?

Context – I do agree with the idea that traffic laws offenders must be heftily penalized.

Well, I believe that...........

Question – Are students studying in a hostel more disciplined than those studying at home?

Context – well, I believe that students develop self discipline at an early age in a hostel.

I do share the same view that.........

Question – Do you think that people who commit murder should be given death penalty?

Context – I do share the same view that they deserve nothing less than death penalty and no mercy should be shown to them who commit such a heinous crime.

I truly subscribe to the view that........

Question – Do you think children should not be educated in schools where medium of instruction is not their mother tongue?

Context – Though I understand the importance of English in the modern world, I believe that creative thinking of kid develops only in his mother tongue so I truly subscribe to the view that they should not be sent to the schools where they are taught in English or any language other than their mother tongue.

Nobody can deny the fact that..........

Question – Do you think movie stars are enjoying more attention than they actually deserve?

Context – Nobody can deny the fact that media nowadays gives undue attention to film stars.

I express my solidarity with the idea that...........

Question – Do you think national symbols should not be allowed to be used during sports tournaments?

Context – I express my solidarity with the idea that national symbols should not only be not allowed but their use should be banned in sports tournament.

I stand by the notion that............

Question – Do you believe that religions divide people in place of uniting them?

Context – I stand by the notion that religions are creating more divisions among people. Actually they should unite the people and bring about peace and harmony in the world.

I honestly admit my approval to the belief that................

Question – Are mothers better at parenting than fathers?

Context – I honestly admit my approval to this traditionally held belief that mother can prove to be a better parent than fathers.

Who would disagree with the fact that...........

Question – Were people in past happier than what we are today?

Context – Who would disagree with fact that people in the past were not only happier but used to lead more secure and fulfilling life?

I don't mind stating that..............

Question – Do you think that parties in power are not doing enough for environment across the world?

I don't mind stating that they in place of protecting environment indulge in damaging it. The cunning nexus between politicians and industrialists is mainly responsible for this sorry state of affairs.

I support the idea of......

Question- Are you in favour of making sports a compulsory subject at a school level?

Context – I support the view that sports should be made compulsory part of school syllabus.

I am in complete favour of........

Question – Do you think that animals are not treated well in your society?

Context – I am in complete favour of the view expressed by you. We exploit them in a great way and violate their basic rights too for our vested interests.

I hold an unshakable belief/opinion in.............

Question - It is generally said that money invested in the construction of religious places are simply the wastage of fund. What do you say?

Context – I hold an unshakable opinion that there are many more areas than simply erecting gigantic temples where money needs to be invested for the betterment of society.

I firmly assert that..........

Question – Is it the responsibility of the society to take care of its elderly people?

Context – I firmly assert here that society must take care of those elderly people, who do not lead secure and dignified life, not all.

I am quite affirmative that............

Question – Do you think people are not very serious about the protection of environment?

Context – I too am quite affirmative about this since people are often seen damaging the eco system simply to fulfil their vested interests.

To express disagreement

I do not buy the argument that........

Question – Do you think all religious people always have high moral standards in life?
Context – I believe that all the religions in the world teach us love and peace but I don't buy the argument that all followers are always the people of high moral values.

I completely disagree with the idea that........

Question – Do you think all politicians are corrupt?
Context – I completely disagree with the idea that all politicians are corrupt. It is inappropriate to blame entire political class because there are many who are incorruptible and discharge their duties so well.

I here express my complete disagreement to what you said in regard to..........

Question - Do you think zoos serve no purpose and hence should be banned?
Context - I here express my complete disagreement to what you just said in regard to the purpose of a zoo because it entertains kids and give us a platform to know animal behaviour.

Honestly speaking, my perception differs from what you have said.........

Question – Do you share the view that old age is always filled with difficulties?
Context – Honestly speaking, my perception differs from what you have said because I think that it is the happiest period of life.

I think very few people would accept the view that..........

Question – Do all the sportsmen play for name and fame nowadays?
Context – I think very few people would accept the view that all sportsmen play for money. Had it been the reality, sportsmen wouldn't have been worshipped like heroes.

I really don't subscribe to the belief that......................

Question – Do you think great sportsmen are always born?
Context – I really don't subscribe to the belief because I think that interest in sports can be cultivated and later a person can be groomed to become a good sportsperson.

I am afraid I don't believe so..........

Question – Do you think that people in big cities are more intelligent than those who live in small cities and villages?
Context – I am afraid I don't believe so because a person's surrounding is not the only factor

which influences his intellectual level.

It appears completely futile and illogical to me to support the view that............

Question – Do you think women are poor decision makers?
Context – It appears completely futile and illogical to me to support that women can not make good decisions. I think gender has nothing to do with good decision making.

I don't find more reasons to stand by what you just said........

Questions – Do you agree with the view that everybody who owns a car actually needs it?
Context – I don't find more reasons to stand by what you just said because owning a car is more a question of sophistication than that of a need.

This view contradicts to what I believe..........

Question – Do you think technology has done more harm than good to human life?
Context – The view contradicts to what I believe because I am an open advocate of the use of technology. Technology never harms us but it is we, the users who use technology in the bad way that it becomes dangerous.

I beg to differ from what you just said because.........

Question - Do you think creative artists do not get enough importance in society?
Context – I beg to differ from what you just said because it is far from the reality.

I do not support the view that............

Question - Do you think employees in public sector tend to be less innovative and more lethargic than those in private sector?
Context – I do not support the view that people in public sector are less innovative because it is because of them that most of the public sector undertakings make huge profit.

To express partial agreement or disagreement

Not completely, but to a certain extent I would like to agree with..........

Question – Do you think movies corrupt the youth?
Context – Not completely, but to a certain extent I would like to agree with the fact that movies corrupt the youth because some youngsters may fail to see the artistic part of movie making and enjoy scenes of sex, violence and crime.

True, but another side is equally true that.........

Question -Do you agree that people will not watch movies in the future?
Context – True, but another side is equally true that popularity of movies has been rising recently because movies are the best way to unwind in busy lives of people. People will continue to watch movies for relaxation regardless of the effectiveness of a story.

Absolutely but I can't disregard second aspect that..........

Question – Do famous people have equal right over their private life as common people have?
Context – Absolutely but I can't disregard second aspect that they are answerable to society. They can not indulge into doing anything they wish in the name of individual freedom.

It is not less than a dilemma but I will go for the first view.........

Question – Do films have negative or positive effects on society?
Context – This question is not less than a dilemma but I will go for the first view because films are nothing but the expression of reality in an imaginative way. It is completely up to the discretion of the viewer how to interpret it.

I am really oscillating between the two but here I support..........

Question – What is your view about allowing women to work outside? Is it good or bad?
I am really oscillating between the two but here I support the view that they should be given that freedom to work outside. How can society deny them the right to explore their worth?

Both are equally important but I will here support........

Question – Where should government spend more money? To protect environment or to generate more opportunities of employment?
Context – Both are equally important but I support environment since it is a global issue, it has be given a priority.

It is possible that you are right but I am bit sceptical about it.........

Question – Do you share the view that writers are undervalued in our society?
Context – It is possible that you are right but I am bit skeptical about it because good writers enjoy huge status in society.

The view appears good but I am not totally convinced about it………

Question – Do you believe that formal education should start early at the age of four in the world of competition?

Context – The view appears good but I am not totally convinced about the idea of early schooling. I think it will deprive children of their right to enjoy childhood.

I hope it is true but the fact is not so…….

Question – Do you think people nowadays are as happy as they used to be in the past?
Context – I wish it were true but the fact is not so as life is so stressful nowadays.

To state causes for problems and situations

The major reason is.........

Question – Why do some people oppose capital punishment even for serious crimes?
Context – The major reason is their firm belief and strong faith in the essential goodness of humans.

.................is usually blamed for this.

Question – Why do you think youngsters do not prefer to live in joint family?
Ideological differences with elders are usually blamed for this social change.

..................is undisputedly believed to be the main reason for..........

Question – Why do some people keep pets?
Context – Loneliness is undisputedly believed to be the main reason for this.

I can point the finger at...................

Question – Why do you think more and more people nowadays prefer to remain single?
Context – I can point the finger at the ever increasing influence of western society.

............also contributes substantially to ....

Question – Why do terrorist activities take place now and then in the world?
Context – Lapse in security arrangements contribute substantially to this sorry state of affairs.

I can't disregard the..............

Question – Why do people buy the things even though they do not need them?
Context – There may be so many reasons but I can't disregard the aggressive marketing done by the companies to lure the consumers.

...................is the breeding ground of.............

Question – What are the causes of air pollution?
Context – Increasing number of private vehicles is the breeding ground of this issue.

............can't escape an accusing eye.

Question – Why do some birds and animals have become extinct?
Context – Government can't escape an accusing eye in this regard because it is the failure on the part of the parties in power to lay down powerful laws to protect some really endangered animals and birds.

Thanks to…………, the ……………has increased.

Question – Why do some people still suffer from malnutrition?
Context – Thanks to poverty and poor policies of government, the rate of malnutrition has been increasing.

Accusing fingers are usually raised at………

Question – Why is corruption thriving despite having strict laws in place?
Context – Accusing fingers are usually raised at the vicious administrative system which not only breeds but encourages corruption.

It is allegedly said that……….

Question - Why has obesity become a common health problem nowadays?
Context – It is allegedly said that sedentary lifestyle and less exercise result into obesity.

To offer solutions

Stringent measures should be taken to................

Question – How can we protect the environment?
Context – Stringent measures should be taken to punish all those who damage our eco system.

Strict laws should be framed to.............

Question – What should be done to curb increasing crime rate?
Context – Strict laws should be framed to punish all those who indulge into criminal activities.

Remedy is...........

Question – How can the public transportation be promoted?
Context – The remedy is to ensure the frequency and regularity of vehicles.

One must................

Question – How can one keep himself fit?
Context – One must do exercise regularly and eat nutritious food.

............should be introduced.

Question – How can corruption be curbed?
Context – New laws should be introduced to combat corruption.

We ought to.........

Question- How can we in our capacity as an individual reduce air pollution?
Context – We ought not to use vehicles until and unless there is a real need to do so.

Government has to...............

Question – What is the best way to remove poverty?
Context – Government has to invite foreign companies to invest in our country to generate more and more opportunities of employment.

It is impossible without............

Question – Can you suggest some ways to keep children fit and disease free?
Context – It is impossible without the cooperation of people in implementing some

health related policies of government.

The need of an hour is...............

Question – In what ways can we fight the menace of drug abuse among youngsters?
Context – The need of an hour is to make them aware of the dire consequences of this malady.

Due attention must be given to..............

Question – How can we promote tourism?
Context – There are many ways but I think due attention must be given to maintain the cleanliness of the tourist places.

Nothing will help until and unless...........

Question – Can you suggest some measures to make people more sensitive towards the issue of domestic violence against women?
Context – Nothing will help until and unless women themselves learn to be self protective and aware.

Efforts should be directed towards...........

Question – How can we keep our family united in modern time?
Context – Efforts should be directed towards increasing communication among all the members and enough space should be given to all to lead their life in their own terms in such a manner that it doesn't affect larger family interests.

To list consequences

It leads to..........

Question – What are possible results of uncontrolled migration towards cities?
Context – There are many but it certainly leads to unemployment and traffic congestion.

An inevitable outcome of this problem will be...............

Question – What will happen if the trend of excessive consumerism continues in the same manner?
Context – An inevitable outcome of this problem will be the negative effects on environment.

It is bound to give rise to............

Question – What will the possible consequences of deforestation be?
Context – It is bound to give rise to air pollution, noise pollution, depletion of ozone layer and desertification.

Some more expressions

The dire consequences will be...................

This problem is likely to breed newer issues like...........

It will result into...........

The issue will create more complications like..............

The worst possible outcome can be..........

There can not be worse consequence than................

To express satisfaction/happiness

I am always excited about………………

Question – Do you like parties?
Context – I am always excited about attending and arranging parties. I really love them.

I always feel pleasant about……..

Question –Do you like spending more time with kids?
Context – I always feel pleasant about spending time with kids.

It gives me an immense satisfaction to……………

Question – Do you like to help others?
Context – It gives me an immense satisfaction in doing so because there is a greater joy in seeing others happy.

I feel a deep sense of happiness in……….

Question – Do you pray everyday?
Context – I pray everyday sine I feel a deep sense of happiness from within.

I really love to…………

Question – Do you watch movies?
Context - I really love to watch movies.

Some more expressions

My heart goes out to……………
It truly excites me to……………
I am bowled over by…………
It never displeases me to…………
It deeply pleases me……………
My heart gets filled with ecstasy when……...........
It given me an extreme joy whenever……………….
I find it really appealing to……………..
It interests me most when………………….
I am at my best when……………
………………takes me to the peak of joy.
It really thrills me to………….
It enthralls me to………………

I find it truly enchanting................
I love to be captivated in........

To give an individual opinion

If I speak my mind out then...........
I hold the view that...............
In my capacity as an individual, I can say that...........
I firmly believe that...............
I would rather say that............
It is my clear standpoint that............
I state that..........
I say it affirmatively that...........
I insist that.............
I share the view that............
I am of the view that............
I strongly opine that..........
It is my honest opinion that............
I admittedly say that........
I critically say that............
As far as my experience goes......
As far as my knowledge is concerned.......

To make additions to the idea or To reiterate something

Let me not forget here to say that.............
I would like to make an addition.............
Apart from this........
Besides this..........
More than what I said earlier...
It should also be mentioned here that................
In the context to what I just said...............
If I refer to what I mentioned earlier, I say that........
To strengthen my main idea, I say that............
It is completely in relevance to the main idea that..........
Let me reiterate differently............
I would like to add here................
In regard to what I stated earlier, I would like to say that.........

To give an example

For example…………
For instance……….
In support to what I just said……….
Let me mention here…………….
It reminds me of one experience in my life…………
To strengthen my view, I quote here……..
In justification to what I just said………..
To justify my view………….
I would like to quote………

Will Taking the IELTS test make me more desirable? And other Myths about the test.

IELTS has been the leading test of English language assessment now for nearly 22 years. It is trusted by High Commissions/Embassies, government agencies, companies and educational institutions around the world to show a person's ability to manage in the English Language. Because the benefits of getting the desired score are significant and can really change someone's life. IELTS is called a 'high stakes' test. Over the years, this reputation has led to many rumors and misconceptions/myths to circulate about the test in India. We call them myths as they have been passed down like stories from one person to another taking up a lot of time, energy and creating anxiety. Here are some of the most frequently heard rumours.

MYTHS AND FACTS

1. AT paper is easier when there is a combined AT and GT date.

The facts: Before it actually appears on a test paper, every question that appears in an IELTS paper has to go through very long and rigorous checking processes for validity, reliability, cultural sensitivity, level of difficulty /ease etc. The Questions are trialled and analyzed statistically, and it can take a long time from when a question is first conceived to when it appears on an actual test, if it ever does! Once a question is seen as 'fit', it will be included on a test paper at some point of time. Sometimes test takers think that doing the test at a time when there are a lot of candidates, i.e. on a GT/AT date, rather than AT only, means the process will be easier, or that the examiners will be more generous. Not so- the standards remain the same, whatever the date and regardless of the number of candidates present.

2. GT is easier than AT

The facts: As mentioned above, the level of difficulty or ease is standardized across both papers. However, as the GT module looks at everyday language activities rather than academic subjects, you may be more familiar with the vocabulary or able to identify better with the situations, so it may 'feel' easier to you.

3. Examiner Myths

There are many myths about examiners for speaking and writing, and a few of the ones we hear are:

IDP Examiners are lenient when marking the writing scripts, or British Council writing examiners 'always' mark low

BC Speaking examiners are 'rigid' and do not take into account the candidate's difficulties/background

If you are from Kerala the examiner marks you down

Examiners in some cities are kinder and give you better marks

I have to say exactly what the examiner wants to hear otherwise I will not get a high score.

The facts: All examiners, globally, go through the same rigorous training process. They are monitored regularly and have to take a test in order to ensure they mark in the same way and to the same standards according to clearly defined criteria and objective marking schemes. Examiners also have to learn about the procedures for doing the speaking test, which are also same globally. They are not permitted to make up questions or change the topics depending on the person in front of them.

Therefore, you can be sure that examiners mark in exactly the same way throughout India, and indeed throughout the world!

4. Venue/test city effects

The test is easier in Jalandhar or Kerala than in other places in India.

Taking the test in smaller cities will give you more marks as examiners are lenient

Appearing for test in North India will ensure a higher score as compared to other regions.

The facts: We have seen that many people travel from Punjab to Kerala or from other parts of India to Jalandhar etc. This is a wonderful way to see this beautiful country, but less relaxing than going on holiday. If you feel it might be easier in one place, perhaps you"ll be more confident and relaxed, so this might help you in your performance. However, both the GT and AT test papers are identical on any one test date throughout the country. Even more importantly, they are the same for the region, so even going to Singapore or Sri Lanka won't make a difference! The fact is that IELTS examination is a standardised , global test. Students taking the examination on the time zone, regardless of whether it is in Bhutan, Bangalore or Bangkok will face exactly the same sets of questions and tasks. This is not a coincidence, but deliberately organized to ensure reliability, security and standardisation across the IELTS community and time-zones.

5. Change to the IELTS test

Two of the main rumours we hear commonly regarding changes to IELTS are:

There will be negative marking introduced shortly.

The IELTS test pattern is going to change soon

The facts: The test has now been in existence for over twenty years, with more than 1.5 million test being administered globally every year. There are always rumours about possible changes to the test, and from time to time there have been some. This is part of the evolutionary process and natural development of any test. The changes are, at times, a result of feedback from users and takers, and other times made to try to make it more relevant to the changing world we live in.The last major changes that occurred with the IELTS were the re-introduction of half-band for scoring and more detailed pronunciation criteria. There is absolutely no truth in either of the rumour that negative marking is going to be introduced, or that the format is going to change. In general, unlike the GMAT and other tests which may have negative marking, the UK exam system does not generally work this way, so this is unlikely to happen with IELTS in the near future!
Although there are no proposed changes to the structure or format of the test, the next major change will be the introduction of computer-based IELTS sometime over the next 18 months two years.

6. IELTS will vanish in 2 years since the demand is decreasing

The fact: After more than 20 years and with the increasing number of test takers, there is nothing on the horizon to indicate IELTS is not going to be around for many more years. There are other test options available now, and competition is a good thing as it ensures continued quality of products and service. However, there is currently no other test available that is fit for the purpose in the same way that IELTS is and which also has the same international recognition as IELTS.

7. If I get someone else to take the test form me, I'll get a visa based on their score.

The facts: There are many unethical individuals exploiting the desperation of ordinary people wishing to improve their lives in another country. Individuals have sometimes paid many hundreds of thousands of rupees to try to get someone to take the test for them promising to guarantee a band score. Apart from the fact that the methods used to do this are often illegal, as they might involve false documents etc., there is no guarantee that you will get your visa. There are sophisticated ways of detecting if someone has cheated, and even though it may not be discovered at a later time, maybe even months after the test date. This information may then be made available to partners such as the UKBA and Australian High Commission, affecting the individual's chances of ever getting a visa for the that country.

We would advise you to use your money wisely for your own long term good rather than in trying to get around the system! Wait a few extra months and spend money on improving your English instead. This will mean that you have a better level of English and be able to get a visa legally which in turn will help you to get a better job once you do get to your destination country. It will also mean a better lifestyle with greater opportunities in your chosen country and consequently enable you to integrate better.

8. If you have a speech difficulty like a stammering problem the examiner will cut your test short

The facts: This is completely untrue. Examiners are trained to manage all kinds of situations and special cases. If you have difficulty such as a speech, auditory or visual impairement, you should contact the British Council center you are registering with and inform them as soon as possible. You will need to provide a medical certificate detailing the difficulties your condition can cause. We will then offer you the correct circumstances for you to able to perform to your best ability.

9. If you speak with an 'accent' you will get better scores in speaking

The facts: IELTS is a test that assesses your ability to communicate in English. As it tests international English, there are many different accents used in the listening test, which reflect the reality you are likely to face wherever you are using the language. Therefore, it does not matter what kind of accent you speak with as long as it is easy for the listener to understand you. You are not expected to change your accent for the IELTS test. The marks for pronunciation are for clarity, fluency and your ability to express feelings through the pauses and intonation you use. Try to focus on speaking clearly at a natural pace so that the examiner can understand you easily. Practicing your English every day and listening to people with different accents will help you to understand & speak English better.

10. There's an auspicious day for you to take the test

The facts: If you believe an astrologer can help you to find a lucky day for you to take the test, then of course you should go and seek advice, but the test is benchmarked to be of the same level of ease/difficulty every session. To ensure this, all questions go through statistical analyses for level of ease or difficulty. It might appear easier sometimes if there are articles included on things which you are interested in or have studied about as the topics and vocabulary might be more familiar to you.

11. A band 7 will get you a better husband or wife/make you more desirable

The facts: Well, I'm not sure you'll get a better person, but looking at the matrimonial ads in newspapers you might find that if you have a band 7, your chances of getting a partner may improve, so perhaps it'll increase your net worth in the marriage market and make you more desirable. Following on from this, things we desire are more attractive to us anc therefore, could be seen as more beautiful!

(**Source:** IELTS examNews - a quarterly News Paper By British Council)

IMPORTANT NOTE

- Interviews 1 to 25 have an extra ordinarily good level of language.

- Students educated in English medium schools will find them very interesting.

- For others, they are the great source of impressive and relevant words.

- The vocabulary used in these interviews is of great significance especially for IELTS speaking module.

- Collect those pearls and prepare them to become a good speaker.

- Interviews 26 to 50 have the language bit simpler than the language used in interviews 1 to 25.

- Students educated in non-English medium schools will find them very interesting.

- Others will appreciate ideas expressed and pertinent use of cohesive devises.

- The vocabulary used in these interviews is not so difficult but rather it is simple and effective.

- You can learn the one great thing from this segment and it is how to make an effective use of your knowledge resources.

Interview 1

Part One:

Q: 1 Do you like shopping? Why?

I am not shopoholic but, whenever I need to buy anything I make a list of the things to be bought and go shopping. However, when I go shopping I buy a good number of things at a time.

Q: 2 Where and with whom do you go shopping?

With my friends and sometimes with my parents, I go shopping near my house. There is a big shopping mall just ten-minute walk from my home.

Q: 3 How often do you go shopping?

I generally go shopping twice in a month but if I need to buy anything, I go shopping anytime. And during festivals, I tend to go shopping more often.

Q: 4 Do you prefer any particular time for shopping? Why?

Normally I prefer to go shopping in evening as I am free in the evening. Besides, my friends are also free so they can accompany me. During summer afternoons, the sun is beating down and I don't prefer to go out in the sun.

Q: 5 What other facilities are available in your town for recreation?

In Baroda, there are a number of things for recreation. For example, we have a good number of public gardens and parks and a couple of swimming pools as well. Moreover, there are some hobby classes in the town.

Q: 6 What kinds of hobbies do you pursue in your leisure?

In my leisure I play volleyball, chess and badminton sometimes. Apart from these, I go to a gym to pump iron. Occasionally I dabble in painting also.

Part Two:

Talk about a thing you would like to buy in the near future.
Say...
What the thing is and what it looks like...

What purpose it serves and...

Why you want to buy it...

Ans:

A person's desire for luxuries never ends. The thing I would like to buy in the near future is a bungalow by the river Sabarmati. The bungalow I intend to buy should have a balcony overlooking the gleaming river so that I can treat myself to a beautiful vista every day. I can contemplate the reflection of the sun on the river in the morning or the evening and at night I can observe the cool moon on the river. Besides, I would like to feel the cool breeze passing over the river and see birds skimming over the river. My bungalow should have two storeys. The ground floor should comprise a spacious living hall, two cosy bed rooms, a silent study room, a kitchen and a washroom. There should be a big spacious hall and two bed rooms on the first floor. And I would like to get the walls painted in various colours.

People misleadingly believe that a house only shelters a person. Nonetheless, I hold that a house not only shelters us but it provides us with space to be ourselves without any reserve. Besides, our house speaks who we are. Thus, I think not only we make a house but our house also makes us.

It is the tedium and restlessness of life in a so-called posh and densely populated area that has made me want a house far away from the madding crowd. And I think living in such a house will endow me with an opportunity to re-discover myself.

Part Three:

Q: 1 It is said that consumerism has been on rise recently. Do you agree? Why?

I agree that consumerism is increasing nowadays and I see various reasons for it. The main reason is that advancements in science and technology have made our life very much comfortable and easy. On account of automation, people have got rid of a good number of manual tasks and consequently they have got plenty of time to pursue their hobbies and interests. Besides, jobs have become more lucrative and businesses have begun to thrive. So people have more money and little to do, which urges them to splurge money in order to buy happiness.

Q: 2 What harm have we done to the environment while building houses?

While building houses we chop down a lot of trees for space and furniture. Thus deforestation takes place, which makes land arid. Besides, we have exhausted minerals and other non-renewable sources. Furthermore, building more houses leads to congestion and other problems such as pollution and displacement of local faunas.

Q: 3 Do you think nowadays people tend to buy more things than they need? Why?

I do believe that these days people buy more than they need because the average purchasing power of our country has gone up and explosion of media and information makes consumers aware of the best deals. Besides, sometimes advertisements also tempt people into buying something that they do not need. For instance, an advertisement about 50% discount on all purchases can be simply irresistible to a potential customer and he will buy the advertised thing just to avail himself of the discount notwithstanding the fact that the thing bought is of little use to him.

Q: 4 What would happen to buying and selling if there were no media such as television and newspapers?

If there were no media such as television or newspapers, customers would be aware of only a limited number of things and as a result they would not be able to get a good deal. Similarly, companies would not be able to attract a good number of customers because advertising their products requires media. However, a product would sell only by a word of mouth. And I think that it would be better as only a genuine product that deserves a customer's appreciation would sell if there were no media. Besides, if there were no media, a credulous customer would not be beguiled into buying thing of no value.

Q: 5 What is your opinion about allowing foreign companies to invest directly in our country?

Despite a lot of apprehension expressed by a lot of people against foreign direct investment, I am of the opinion that foreign investment will strengthen our country's economy. Because of foreign investment numerous foreign companies come to our country and provide jobs to the youth of our country. Besides, they also collaborate with our country's corporations and introduce quality products at a very low rate. This will ultimately benefit our country's people. However, I think before allowing any foreign company to operate in our country, the past record of the foreign company must be checked for its credibility.

Q: 6 Do you think some corporations harm environment?

Yes, some companies harm environment. For example, poisonous fumes emitted by some factories cause several diseases and deformities. Some effluent released by factories into a river or sea can extinguish endangered species. Apart from air pollution and water pollution, mills also cause noise pollution, which leads to hearing impairment. Though wind energy is considered to have no negative ramifications on environment, some countries have banned wind mills in some areas because setting up wind mills threatens the fauna and flora of virgin terrains.

Interview 2

Part One:

Q: 1 What electronic gadgets do you use every day? Why?

I use many electronic gadgets like a mobile, TV, CD player, a laptop, an iron etc.

Q: 2 Is there any electronic gadget that you cannot do away with?

I think a mobile is such an indispensable gadget because as I have to be in touch with my parents. Wherever I go, I need to carry a mobile with me so that whenever I or they need, we can communicate with each other very easily.

Q: 3 What are other modes of communication apart from talking on the mobile?

Apart from chatting on the mobile, there are various modes of communication such as chatting through the net, sending an email or a snail mail, talking in person. Besides, there are also some non-verbal modes of communication for example touch, sign posts, gesticulation, gestures and various sounds.

Q: 4 How is daily news communicated to people?

It is communicated through news papers, news channels, the radio, the internet, posters, hoardings and through the grapevine.

Q: 5 Which method do you think conveys reliable news? Why?

I guess news conveyed by newspapers is always reliable since journalists have enough time to analyse the news, cross-examine witnesses and thus verify what they are going to report.

Q: 6 What kind of newspapers do you read? Why?

I read The Financial Express as I learn a lot of things from it, which can be helpful in my MBA course. Besides, I also read a local daily as it keeps me abreast of the latest happening in my locality.

Part Two:

Talk about an electronic device that you would like to buy.

Say...

What kind of device it is...

Why you want to but it...

What kind of features you want in the device...

Ans:

The electronic device I would like to buy is a laptop. As I live in a hostel away from my parents and friends back in my hometown, a laptop with the internet connection can help me keep in touch with them. Besides, a laptop can be of great use in my studies, because the information and pictures that I need for my college projects and assignments can be gleaned from various websites. Moreover, a laptop can also serve as a music system. I can plug in a pair of earphones and listen to mellifluous music in order to recharge my batteries. I agree that indulging too much insocial networking sites can jeopardise study, but a judicious use of these websites to exchange information and views with other scholars enriches our knowledge. Thus, I would like to use social networking sites for a better cause. However, I will take care not to allow social networking sites to impinge on my studies.

At present i do not require a laptop with a very advanced configuration. As per my needs I would like to buy a laptop that has some features such as an in-built camera, in-built speakers, two GB RAM, windows 7, and core dual processor. And last but not the least, it should have a long-lasting battery.

Part Three:

Q:1 How do you think electronic gadgets have influenced our life?

Electronic gadgets have become an inevitable part of modern life since they are used in all fields, be it education, medicine, engineering, communication or advertisement. Electronic gadgets have streamlined communication across various strata. For example, through the internet one can keep in touch with his relatives and friends who live abroad. In public sectors such as banking, ticket booking and opinion poll, age old rigmarole has been superseded by online banking, online ticket booking and online opinion poll. The shift from "in line" to "online" has made electronic gadgets like laptops, mobiles and computer very popular.

Q:2 Do you think there is any less welcome side of electronic gadgets?

Yes. Like every coin, electronic gadgets too have positive as well as negative sides. Sometimes a beep of a mobile during an important meeting can divert the speaker's attention. Besides, some unsolicited advertisements keep hassling us no matter where we are and what the time is. Some unscrupulous people develop some software to hack somebody's important password such as banking password and siphon off somebody else's money into their own account.

Q:3 What kind of technology do you think will be developed in future?

I believe that necessity is the mother of all inventions. Thus new technologies will be developed according to our needs in future. For instance, in metropolitan cities the problem of traffic congestion is looming large. So some people may invent some flying machines for short distances. Besides, now that we have been exhausting petroleum, they might invent some technology to make petroleum artificially from other materials.

Q:4 Do you think that elderly people are less interested in technology than young generation is?

It is interesting to make comparison between the popularity of technology among youngsters and the popularity of technology among grey population. In cosmopolitan cities and among educated people it is found that elderly people are interested in technology as much as youngsters are. However, in rural societies elderly people do not show any interest in technology because they are totally unaware of advancements in technologies. Nonetheless, children from villages do show keen interest in new gadgets and technologies.

Q:5 Does technology influence our life style?

Yes, by all means. Because of automobiles we can easily travel anywhere and internet and other communication technologies help us in passing our messages to anywhere. Thus we don't need to walk and our life has become sedentary, which causes a number of problems including obesity and diabetes.

Q:6 Do you think we can stop being too much dependent on technologies?

Though it is difficult but it is not utterly impossible to become less dependent on technology as there are some daily chores that can be done manually for example washing clothes, sweeping the floor. The use of power-point presentation may be time-saving and more effective but it makes us crippled when the light goes off. So if we use some other means such as chalk and talk for presentation, we can become independent of technology. Nonetheless, I think it is virtually impossible to become absolutely independent of technology because it has become the integral part in our life-style.

Interview 3

Part One

Q: 1 what kind of entertainment do you like? Why?

As I am one of literati, I enjoy reading and writing literature, especially in English language because it helps me in developing my insight into literature and further inspires me to create literature of grand style. Besides, I occasionally go to the cinema.

Q: 2 What kinds of film do you enjoy watching?

I enjoy watching historical films as they enrich my knowledge and give me a flavour of various cultures of different countries and times. Further, I also enjoy watching romantic films provided they are not sentimental type, because romantic films infuse optimism in me. And when i desperately need a hearty laugh, I watch comedies.

Q: 3 Who do you normally go with to watch a film?

It depends on my mood. If I'm in a mood of having unlimited fun, definitely I prefer the company of my friends but if I want to spend some memorable moments I go to the cinema with my girlfriend.

Q: 4 Is there any particular cinema that you prefer? Why?

Generally, I prefer going to Nataraj cinema, as it's just five-minute walk from my hostel, where I'm currently living. Besides, it's really affordable and comparatively, there is less rush.

Q: 5 Do you enjoy living in the hostel? Why?

I enjoy living in the hostel indeed as I am always in company of my friends and we help each other in various things such as academics, sports, university election and cooking. Besides, it inculcates us with a feeling of solidarity.

Q: 6 What do you do when you miss your parents?

When I miss them, I call them or I chat with them through the net. And three times in a month I pay a visit to them.

Part Two:

A film that you saw last.

Say...

Where and when you saw it...

With whom you saw it...

What the story was...

Whether you liked it and why...

Ans:

I am not much of a theatre-goer but whenever I get a company of congenial friends I do not mind watching a film with them. The film I saw last is "Goya's Ghost", a British film, I guess. As it was a leisurely Sunday we were just wondering how to pass the day and one of my friends suggested watching a film on TV at his home. So we all friends drove to his place and watched the film.

The film is set in old times when the church held supreme power and exposes depravity in papacy. There is a pope who warns his disciples against some Jews who are living under the guise of Catholics. The pope describes some customs the Jews follow and tells his disciples to identify Jews living among them. The disciples happen to be dining at a tavern. They notice a girl who refuses to eat pork. The disciples remember the pope saying that Jews abstain from pork. Thus the disciples suspecting the girl to be a Jew disguised as a Catholic report the phenomenon to the pope, who sends his people to arrest the girl. When the girl is produced before the pope, he puts her to "the question" i.e. he tries to elicit from the girl the answer he wants by torturing her. She is hanged upside down stark naked but she does not confess to practising Jewish customs and maintains that she is born of Catholic parents. However, she admits that her great grand father was a Jew but he converted to Catholicism. This becomes a solid reason for the fanatic pope to torment and mortify her more. When the girl's father comes to know about her predicament he takes help of his friend called Goya, who is a renowned painter. Goya often makes portraits of the royal family and is on good terms with the king and the pope. Through Goya, the girl's father invites the pope to dinner. During dinner the girl's father asks the pope if he has ever been put to "the question" himself. The pope says ,"No." The girl's father asks the pope further if the church still believes in a brutal custom called "the question" and whether the statements elicited by force can be true. The pope says, "If one has not sinned, God will grant him the fortitude to stand the question." The girl's father seizes upon this opportunity and immediately hangs the pope upside down from a fan and puts him to "the question". Further, he forces the pope to sign a document that reads, "I, the pope, am a bastard progeny of an orang-utan and a chimpanzee." After getting this document signed he tells him that he will return the document to him the day his daughter gets home and lets the pope go. However, the pope tortures the girl more ruthlessly and even rapes her and later bears a daughter. As she cannot be proved to be a Jew, she is released. But when she comes out of the jail, all her family members are dead and she has nowhere to live. She becomes a destitute with a famished daughter in her arms. Nonetheless, in the long run the depravity of the pope is exposed and he is humiliated and hanged in public. The movie ends with the girl carrying her daughter in her arms and running after the donkey-cart in which the pope's corpse was being conveyed. And the background song sung by children makes audience lament on the delayed justice.I just love the story because it unravels hypocrisy and moral degradation set in so-called religious people.

Part Three:

Q: 1 Do you think films have positive or negative effects on us?

Most of films are made in such a way that their interpretation depends on audience and therefore interpretation varies from person to person. It is up to a viewer what he should take from a film. To illustrate this, a reflective viewer finds a realistic depiction of an emerging actress in the film "Dirty Picture", whereas some people only watch sensuous scenes of the film. A film that makes us think and draws our attention to some issues and problems ultimately has a positive effect on us. However, there are some seedy and steamy films that pander to voyeurs in particular. And I think they can never have any desirable effect on audience.

Q: 2 Do films corrupt youngsters?

How can any outer influence corrupt us until and unless we desperately want to get corrupted? Films just reflect reality in an imaginative way. I agree that there are some films that show lots of sex, violence and drug abuse. However, this sort of film is advised to be seen under parent's guidance. Moreover, I am of the opinion that if youngsters want to pick up some bad habits, they do not have to depend on films because they have other ways of getting exposure to undesirable things.

Q: 3 How has making of a film changed over the period of time?

The type of film made long back, say, four decades back differs a lot from the type of film produced nowadays in terms of technology, music, aesthetic sense, fashion and culture. In past film were black and white, while nowadays films are not only colourful but three dimensional also. The musical instrument used in past were very simple but a wide range of musical instruments are used in modern films. Talking about Indian cinemas, the culture portrayed in old films is rare. Old films showed the society suppressed by rigid rules and regulations. Besides, the protagonist belonged to a poor family. At present, these things are not found in Indian cinemas.

Q: 4 How does a film reflect the culture of the country it was made in?

A film sometimes becomes an informal mouthpiece of its country's culture. For example, American films often show a protagonist who relentlessly and single-handedly fights all odds and achieves victory. This indicates that American culture celebrates courage, vigour and individualism. Similarly, popular Indian films showing victory of a joint family over a nuclear family reflects significance of joint families in India. Besides, there are some films narrating a mythological character, which explain some customs of the country. For example Hollywood has produced a good number of films explaining "the fall of man" and "original sin". Apart from themes, dressing of actors also gives a glimpse of the culture. And actually, films play a major role in spreading fashion.

Q: 5 Do you think there should be stricter censorship on films or films should be given more freedom of expression?

I am against any kind of censorship, except something blatantly preposterous and capable of causing a great harm to humanity. Some ingenious film-makers make some films to expose corruption and depravity prevailing in a so-called civilised society. Common people can learn a lot and benefit from this kind of film but this kind of film is ultimately banned as it raises voice against vested interests. I firmly believe that ban on this kind of film keeps common people ignorant of venality of their so-called leaders. However, no film-maker should try to impinge on privacy of public figures.

Q: 6 Do you prefer watching a film or reading a book? Why?

It is an interesting question. My preference for reading a book or watching a film depends on the subject. For example if it is a romance, I prefer watching a film because a melodious song makes romantic atmosphere more realistic. On the other hand if it is a historical story, I prefer reading a book so that I can easily remember names of places and characters as well as important dates. However, if I am to watch a film that is adopted from a book, I prefer going through the book before watching the film.

Interview 4

Part One:

1) What kind of art do people appreciate in your country?

In my country people appreciate various kinds of arts such as paintings, mural, fresco, folk dances, folk songs and dramas based on myths and contemporary issues. Besides, people nowadays show keen interest in architecture. In short, people appreciate both modern and ancient arts in my nation.

2) Describe a dance that is very popular in your locality.

I come from Gujarat, which is well-known for its dance called Garba, which is performed specially during Navaratri, a holy festival of Hindus. There're lots of type of Garba, but Ras is very famous. In Ras, a couple dances carrying a pair of short sticks in their hands and moves them rhythmically with beats of songs. A row of couples dancing in this way rotates on a big ground.

3) Who is your favourite singer? Why?

I admire Abida Parvin's singing as she generally sings spiritual songs such as Kabir's couplets or songs of sufi gurus. Moreover, her voice has a kind of subtle spirituality, which appeals to me and all of her songs have profound meaning.

4) What kind of music did you like when you were a child?

When I was a child, I liked nursery rhymes, lullabies and some Gujarati folk songs. However, I used to listen to songs of Hindi films but they were not my favourites.

5) What kind of music do you dislike?

As I love music with slow beats, I don't like heavy metal music, which sounds very cacophonous to my ears.

6) What advantages do you see in listening to music?

I think listening to music makes us calm and improves our concentration. It is also believed that a certain kind of music has spiritual values. And that's why in past some enlightened seers were also good singers. Listening to spiritual music can infuse us with positive energy.

Part Two:

Speak about your favourite painter.

Say...

Who he is...

How you came to know about him...

Why you like him...

Ans:

Among all types of arts the type that appeals to me very much is visual art. I have a collection of several contemporary and classical paintings at my home, since my grandfather is very much fond of paintings. Among all painters, the painter I like most is Vincent Van Gogh. It was an autumn evening and I was having a stroll in my school campus when I caught a sight of a painting of sunflowers done in wax colour. What fascinates me so much about this painting is its simplicity and sharp contrast created by its dexterous colour scheme. Then I saw a biographical movie about Van Gogh and also read a book titled "The Lust for Life" by Irving Stone. The book and the movie both are fantastic in terms of realistic delineation of Van Gogh's like and make a reader or a viewer feel the agony and ecstasy Van Gogh went through in his life. There are a good number of reasons for my liking him but the foremost reason for my fascination of and reverence to Van Gogh is the fact that he is a rarest of artists who creates his art for himself and not only as per the public demand. I would rather say that he is like a songbird who sings for himself and his song comes from his heart. Besides, it is interesting to note that Van Gogh is such an artist who could not sell his paintings during his life time and fasted in order to save money for colour and canvas. Nonetheless, after his death his paintings started selling like a hot cake and critics as well as students of visual arts became very much curious about his life. I have an impression about him that he was a self-effacing artist and an introvert seeker after the truth. His last wish was to paint the rising sun and he observed the sun rise for a long span of time and ultimately painted the sun rising. However, he committed a suicide after fulfilling his last wish. His extraordinary sensitivity stood in sharp contrast with the ruthlessness of the world.

Part Three:

Q:1 Do you think the painter's profession has been threatened by cameras?

I don't think that technology can pose any threat to a painter's profession because a painter not only paints what it but he paints what there can be, what there has to be, what there will be and what lies hidden deep beneath ostensible reality. And a resourceful painter, in my opinion, can make a wise use of technology to highlight his creativity. Moreover, a camera can take a picture of concrete things only, whereas a painter can paint concrete as well as subtle and intangible things with the same kind of creativity.

Q:2 Do you think these days people have apathy towards arts?

The view I hold is contrary to your statement. Looking at the amount of money youngsters and even elderly people shell out for music, printed t-shirts, learning various kinds of dance and paintings, I can assume that popularity of arts is increasing among people of all ages. And that is why the present generation is desperate to become an artist. Notwithstanding, some classical arts find very few takers in modern times. For example, in painting photo-realism is no longer popular at present, instead surrealism, Dadaism and existentialism are in vogue.

Q: 3 Do you think artists are true representatives of culture?

Yes, I agree to some extent that artists are true representatives of culture because they painstakingly give a creative expression to a society's culture. Though there are some artists who misrepresent and defame one country's culture, most of artists represent their culture faithfully. However, culture being a bigger phenomenon cannot be confined to artists. Even cooks, tailors, barbers, educators, poets and masons can be called true representative of culture as their work mould our taste and life-style.

Q: 4 Sometimes some creative writers and artists allegedly hurt public sentiments. Why do you think they do so?

I guess that some artists do it just as a publicity stunt, whereas some resort to this kind of defamatory acts just to show that they are different from others. However, I believe that there are some artists who are not aware of the traditional values and ethos of a community and they end up unwittingly making something that hurts people's sentiments. I think that they should be made aware of some customs and values they have to abide by, though they are creative artists.

Q: 5 Do arts differ from country to country?

Yes, an art, being a true expression of a country's culture, is bound to differ from country to country. For example in Chinese paintings a shadow of an object is rarely painted whereas in American paintings a shadow is painted in order to make a painting realistic. Another example where I find differences between Greek paintings and Indian paintings is that Greek paintings are more realistic and show keen interest in depicting shapes of muscles, while Indian paintings concentrate more on emotions of figures painted in a painting. However, despite these minor differences, I find a common quality among all arts. And that is they all try to entertain and educate us simultaneously.

Q:6 According to you what does future hold for arts seeing that the current generation is more inclined towards science and commerce?

Though science and commerce faculties attract a great number of students at present, I don't think that the future of arts is bleak. Don't we see youngsters splashing out a lot of money on designer jewellery, interior decoration of their houses, concerts and films? In this era when everybody is obsessed with a good look, students of design schools are in great demand. Besides, we also need good script writers for popular film and prolific copy-writers for advertising companies. And we need poet laureates who can sing our nation's proud saga. If there were no arts, the world would look like an incongruous crowd of specialists who fail to understand each other.

Interview 5

Part One:

1) How do you relax yourself?

To relax myself, I go out for a walk with my friends or watch a film or sometimes listen to music.

2) What subjects did you study at your school?

At my school I studied maths, English, history, painting, music, social sciences, geography, civics, Indian culture and civilisation and logic.

3) What subject did you like most? Why?

Though I enjoyed all the subjects offered at my school, the subject I liked most and still like most is logic because it teaches us how to think properly. Besides, careful study of logic develops in us abilities to analyse, predict, prove and refute.

4) Who was your favourite teacher at your school? Why?

At my school my favourite teacher was Dr R C Patel because he did not only teach us the prescribed curricula but also encouraged and motivated us to explore the world around us. Further, his teaching involved demonstration, experiments, examples and easy explanation, which distinguished him from other teachers.

5) What subject or subjects did you hate at your school? Why?

At my school I hated history most because I think it compels us to remember unnecessary

this, nowadays discotheques are abuzz with "Kolaveri" even though most youngsters do not understand the words of the song. Nonetheless, if media do not provide a platform to an artiste, people will take no notice of him or her, though he or she may be an artist of high calibre.

Q:6 Many people criticise contemporary songs as cheap songs. What is your view on this?

I think music cannot be cheap or lofty but lyrics can be sometimes of cheap quality as they cater to the masses. For example, some songs of Hindi films have absurd lyrics and I really wonder if the song writer himself can understand his songs. Though these lyrics are poor in literary qualities, they entertain a certain type of people. Thus this kind of songs fulfil their purpose. But we cannot make a too sweeping generalisation that all contemporary songs are of poor quality because there are some songs that appeal to refined tastes.

Interview 6

Part One:

1) Who is your ideal? Why?

My ideal is nobody but myself because I live in present and I accept happily what I am. Besides, I think imposing somebody else's ideology or persona on yourself is the greatest humiliation of yourself.

2) What qualities do you admire in a person? Why?

The qualities I admire in a person include honesty, truthfulness, sincerity, industry, good sense of humour, passion for knowledge and companionship because these are the very qualities that distinguish human beings from other species and make a human life the most coveted boon.

3) What qualities would you like to inculcate in your children? Why?

I'd like to inculcate my child with desirable qualities such as solidarity, honesty, a keen sense of inquiry and passion for knowledge because a child with a keen sense of inquiry and passion for knowledge can pursue his dreams better and consequently he is more likely to realise his dreams.

4) What kind of people do you think become famous?

I reckon that the people who've done something new in their field become famous, for example, scientists, exceptionally skilled engineers, litterateurs and artists. However, some people also become famous for their physical or mental abilities.

5) What do you usually do at the weekend?

I generally go out with my friends to some parks, the cinema or libraries. Sometimes I also eat out at the weekend.

6) What kinds of films do you see?

My taste in this regard is very different from that of my friends. In the first place, I don't like watching romantic films except it is based on some social issues. I generally prefer films relating to psychology, for example the film "Inception", because I learn a lot about people's behaviour from this kind of films. Moreover, sometimes I also enjoy historical or documentary films.

Part Two:

Speak about a personality who is controversial.
Say...
Who the personality is...
What he did/does...
Why he is controversial...

Ans:

I am of the opinion that most of public figures love to be in the limelight either by their expertise in their field or by any deliberate controversy they have caused. One such personality I know is Osho, who was earlier known as Acharya Rajneesh. After earning a PhD in Philosophy from the University of Sagar, he went to teach in a university in Jabalpur, where his unconventional method of teaching drew everybody's attention. At the age of thirty, Acharya Rjneesh left his job and started conducting meditation camps at various places in India, which earned him fame as an "Acharya" which in English means a "preceptor". He divested a common man of his established believes and got him to question the so-called religions. His denial of marriage as a social institution, acceptance of love as a sublime spiritual energy and scathing attack on the so-called religions and religious Gurus that advocate suppression of mind made him a highly controversial figure. Osho derided and condemned the religions that idolise poverty as a virtue and despise this life but eulogise the life after death. Moreover, a large number of foreigners pouring in his commune in Pune made local people suspicious about him. To cap it all his series of lectures titled

"From Sex to Super Consciousness", in which he expatiated on sublimation of sexual energy, gravely outraged puritans of the society. Nonetheless, it was this series of lectures that made him a formidably controversial figure. Ultimately he became so much controversial that the person reading Osho's books or wearing his beads was subjected to abomination.

Part Three:

Q: 1 Is it true that some emerging personalities deliberately try to cause some controversy around them? Why?

Yes. Driven by the desire for publicity some budding public figures make intentional faux pas just to remain in limelight. For example a budding writer may write something blasphemous about a religious or political leader or an emerging politician may malign another politician. Moreover, controversy is always used as a publicity stunt in film industries. On the other hand, there are some emerging personalities who are not much familiar with traditional values and therefore the controversies caused by them are unintentional. For example, an American actor kissing an Indian actress publicly becomes a controversy though the American actor has never had the faintest idea about it being controversial.

Q: 2 Should controversies be suppressed or should we try to find out causes and solutions for controversies?

I firmly hold the view that suppression is not an answer to any problem. If there is anything wrong in society, we have to find causes for the wrong thing and considering the causes we have to find a solution. For example, if some top brass are corrupt, we must not ignore it. Instead, we should reveal their depravity with help of media. As this kind of corruption is detrimental to public interests, people must be made aware of it. However, there are some minor differences of opinions among a cricket team or stars, which should not be exaggerated as big controversies as they do not affect interests of the masses.

Q: 3 Has the role of mass media changed over the time? How?

I think that it has changed a lot. Earlier people had limited access to media, whereas nowadays people are bombarded with information—both necessary and unnecessary—by media. In past the main purpose of news channel was to keep people abreast of the latest happenings but these days news channels are more interested in advertising various products and make money. Besides, a couple of decades back media worked under some moral obligations but at preset a sting operation has become an easy way to increase viewership, though it may be unethical. The true duty of mass media is to reveal the truth to public, but in this age of exaggerated and spiced up news, I think, mass media have deviated from their main role.

Q: 4 To what extent do you think the news presented by TV channels is reliable?

I don't think that all news given by TV channels is absolutely correct or totally misleading. There are some news programmes that are produced after a rigorous research, which are really reliable—except public opinions about the happening. On the other hand, sometimes news channels have to kill time when there is not much news. And it is during this time that news channels are tempted to exaggerate some insignificant happenings. Besides, as TV channels generally report events and happenings live, journalists have little time to revise a news report, which may not be much reliable.

Q: 5 Have you ever been in controversy? How?

Though I avoid being in controversy, some of my thoughts are many times misunderstood and described as heresy. For example, being an student of English language and literature I have great expectations from my teachers and if I find my teachers incompetent or lacking in knowledge, I unabashedly express my disapproval and dissatisfaction. When I was studying MA English at the Department of English, I came across such a lazy teacher who never evaluated my assignments justly. Besides, I did not find him well-read. So one day I cross examined him by asking some questions on literary criticism but his answer betrayed his ignorance and his image as a doyen of English literature was shattered. He accused me of impertinence, though my manner of asking him questions was very polite. And I became a very controversial student in the class.

Q: 6 What do you think can be causes of controversies?

I am not sure but causes of controversies may include ego, conflict, cultural differences, suppression, rebellion and heresy. Sometimes a simple meeting between people coming from different cultures can spark controversies as they offend each other unintentionally because of their cultural differences. Moreover, some controversies are not controversies at all but they are just a publicity stunt. This holds true especially for a public figure who has been consigned to oblivion. I assume, some apparent controversies are simply used as a red herring to divert people's attention from other important issues.

Interview 7

Part One:

1) Do you welcome or resist a change? Why?

It depends on the type of change. If it is going to spell a disaster for me or my friends and relatives, I'll leave no stone unturned to nip this kind of change in the bud. However, if it's going to prove to be a boon for me and my nearest and dearest, I'll welcome it with open arms.

2) What things or a thing would you like to change in your life?

To tell you the truth, I get up very late, sometimes at ten in the morning and I get late in reaching my college. Therefore, I'd like to develop a habit or getting up early at six o' clock, because it'll enable me to reach my college on time and then I'll not have to face the music.

3) Whom do you consult before making any crucial decision?

Honestly speaking, I make my decision myself. However, before making any decision, I do seek advice from my well-wishers and elderly people in particular as they are more experienced. If a decision pertains to my career, I consult my professors and seniors, while if it pertains to my engagement, marriage etc, I consult my parents.

4) What kinds of decisions do you make without consulting anybody?

If I have to respond to an unexpected situation and I don't have any friends, relatives or well-wishers with me, I make a spontaneous decision on my own. Besides, if i have to deal with some problems caused by a wrong decision made by me, I don't prefer to consult anybody.

5) How do you think your perspective towards life has changed since your childhood?

When I was a child, for me the world was a safe shelter insulated by my parents but as I grew up I moved out of their protection and started learning how to face and solve problems on my own. Now, I believe I am responsible for whatever happens to me, whether it is good or bad. If I have freedom to err, I also have valour to face repercussions.

6) What things do you remember from your childhood?

My childhood had nothing unique to be remembered but whenever I look back at my childhood, what comes to mind is carefree days of innocence and curiosity. I was so much curious to explore the world around me and I didn't have as many responsibilities as I have today.

Part Two:

A positive change in your life.
Say...
What the change is...
When and how it happened...
What effects it has had on you...

Ans:
I read in Paulo Cohelo's 'The Alchemist', "When someone makes a decision, he is really diving into a strong current that will carry him to places he has never dreamed of." During my first perusal of this line, the full realisation of the meaning evaded me but now that it has been six months since I made a crucial decision, the meaning of the sentence is beginning to dawn on me. The decision I made six months ago was to live and work in my hometown, which is a nondescript rural town where past masquerades as future and present is shrouded in oblivion. Before I started living in my hometown I had an illusion that I could control everything around me. In short, I was a real control freak. But in my hometown I realised that nothing is in my hands, not even my own two hands! I was determined to reach work in time but on my way to work my bike stalled and refused to start again. I had to call a lorry and send it to a nearby garage. Worse than this, as there was no rickshaw around I had to walk a long distance to my work and it was raining cats and dogs. And finally when I reached the college where I teach, I looked unkempt and very grungy. Earlier even a single mistake committed by my students or an innocuous comment passed by them drove me mad. But here students seem to be making no efforts to learn and social etiquette is utterly alien to these innocent creatures. Initially I was extremely repelled by the unabashed rusticity displayed by the students here. But then I thought c'est la vie i.e. that is life. Man proposes and God disposes. It is really commendable that my perspective to life has gone through a sea-change. Earlier, I lived as if I were the centre of the universe but now I have realised that I am just a small ripple rising on the ocean of this existence. Earlier I held somebody else responsible for my happiness or sadness but now I find myself responsible for what I am. This change has been caused by my disposition to ruminate about myself and the things around me.

Part Three:

Q: 1 What inspires a person to bring about a positive change in his life?
I think some people, incidents or thoughts inspire a person to strive for a positive change in his life. For example, during my collegiate days, one professor inspired me to read books and ponder over them. Since then I have read more than approximately one thousand books. Moreover, some

critical situation in life also sometimes inspires us to aspire to a positive change. I remember being ridiculed by my classmates for my weak body structure. But their sarcastic remarks compelled me to become physically fit. Lastly, a well-written book can also motivate us to make positive changes in life. For instance, “The Prophet” by Kahlil Gibran is bound to inspire us to rethink life and develop positive attitude.

Q: 2 Some people are not ready to accept any change. What do you think may be responsible for this?

I think a person's liking for his happy past and his unfounded fear of unseen future can deter him from accepting a change. For instance, if I were having a secure job, I would be reluctant to embark upon my own business as I cannot be sure of profit. Moreover, some people suffer from a kind of myopia. Therefore they are not ready to see a thing from other's point of view. And consequently they become pusillanimous. Sometimes, though a person wants a change, his matrix does not allow him to welcome a change. And it is observed that in old age a person becomes averse to any change.

Q: 3 Do political campaigns bring about any positive change? Why?

I don't think political campaigns can cause any welcome change because despite an apparent noble cause for which a campaign is carried out, politicians give priority to their selfish ends. For instance, if a political campaign is carried out in order to make free education available to children, the cause of the campaign is really laudable but the modus operandi involves some red tape, which turn out to be the biggest obstacle in fulfilling the very purpose of the campaign.

Q: 4 Is it true that people are always waiting for a positive change in their life? Does it really come about?

Yes, I think everybody is waiting for some kind of utopia. However, such an utopia does not necessarily always materialise. More than often it proves to be illusive and those who keep waiting for such an utopia are, in fact, wasting their time. I firmly believe that if you want to do something then what you have is this moment. I don't believe in wasting my valuable present for some unseen future.

Q: 5 It is said that there is no right time to do a right thing. How far do you agree with this?

To a great extent, I agree with and appreciate this wise adage. Because by waiting for a right moment, we are simply squandering our present time. For example, if I know that health is wealth and therefore I want to join a gym, then I don't see any point in deferring joining a gym. However, in some circumstances patience is of great importance, especially in time of business crisis. If I am a successful business man, I will never make any hasty decision. But still let me reiterate that a widening chasm between a decision and an action invariably breeds sloth and indecision.

Q: 6 Do you agree that nowadays people are more desperate for a positive change than people in past?

I think that man has been hankering after a positive change down the ages. However, as man's plight becomes severe his thirst for a positive change intensifies. And the present age is rife with tribulation so the modern man is more desperate for a positive change. Further, a good number of seminars and workshops pertaining to positive lifestyle and spiritual development bear a testimony to how desperate the modern man is for a positive change.

Interview 8

Part One:

1) What kinds of civic facilities are available in your town?

I come from Baroda, a cultural and educational hub of Gujarat. Baroda has a lot of civic facilities for its residents, which include a very big garden called Sayaji Baugh for people's recreation, a hospital called SSG Hospital, a museum for people to know about their cultural heritage, wide and clean roads, numerous schools, local buses, malls, an airport, the cinemas and The Maharaja Sayajirao University, which is a renowned institution of higher learning in the country and also in the world.

2) What positive changes do you expect in your town?

First, I'd like my town to have more drinking water, because at present some residents don't get enough drinking water. Further, international flights should be available at the airport so that those who want to go abroad need not go to Ahmedabad. And finally some old cinemas in the town should be revamped.

3) How would you describe the culture of your town?

The culture of Baroda is intellectually charged and provides conducive atmosphere for visual and performing arts. Besides, education occupies a significant place in this culture. Nonetheless, though the culture here sets great store by education, intellectuality and arts, it does not ignore festivity and the joy of life.

4) Tell me something about any recent event in your town.

A few weeks back, there was a cultural feast, for which some renowned singers, painters and litteratureurs came to the town from various parts of the world and enthralled the audience. This programme included singing of sufi songs, exhibition of paintings and talks on culture and literature.

5) Do you like living in a city or a village? Why?

I definitely like living in a city as there are a lot of opportunities for self-development and career, while in a village there're no institutions of higher learning, nor any job opportunities. Besides, in a city a person has individual freedom, that is to say nobody bothers to know what you're doing. Therefore, you have a good deal of privacy, whereas in a village, a person's privacy is often impinged upon by inquisitive country folks.

6) What country would you like to live in? Why?

I'd like to live in England, because I've heard and read that the standard of living there is very high and the country has healthy economy. Besides, there are esteemed universities like the University of Oxford and the University of Cambridge. Further, as lots of people from various countries migrate to England, it has become a melting pot of culture, which means it is tolerant to cultural differences.

Part Two:

A story you heard in your childhood.
Say...
When and from whom you heard it...
What the story is...
What you learnt from it...

Ans:

When I was about ten years old, my grandmother told me a story, which I still remember. The story goes like this. Once there were two friends- a hare and a tortoise. The hare was always boasting about his ability to run fast and made a jest of the tortoise who was very slow. Just to humiliate him, the hare once challenged the tortoise to a race, assuming that the tortoise was going to lose the game. The tortoise accepted the challenge without baulking at the prospect of his defeat. As decided earlier, the two friends met at the ground and started running. Initially, the hare gambolled and ran very fast. But the poor tortoise was walking at a snail's pace. Consequently, the hare reached so far away from the tortoise that when he looked back there was no tortoise in sight.

Besides, on account of running very fast, he was out of breath and very tired. So he decided to have rest under a shady tree. He thought that he would wake up before the tortoise came in sight but he fell so fast asleep that he was just snoring when the slow walking tortoise overtook him. Unfortunately, when he woke up, to his great dismay he noticed that the tortoise was just an inch away from the goal post. He made a desperate attempt to reach the goal post, but in vain. Thus the boastful hare was defeated by the humble tortoise.

This parable, like all other parables, is open to numerous interpretations. However, I learnt two things from the tale-- one, we should never brag about our ability and another, those whose efforts are slow but steady can do better than those whose efforts are sporadic.

Part Three:

Q: 1 Why do people like listening to stories?

I guess they like listening to stories as stories not only entertain them but also educate them. Besides, stories also make them aware of their country's history and their own lineage. It is said that the truth can be better expressed in a story than in a factual statement. Some mysteries of life that seem to be ineffable can be revealed in a story. Apart from this, a story also enriches the language in which it is narrated and demonstrates the narrator's ability to evoke certain emotions, feelings and memories in listeners.

Q: 2 Do you think that nowadays with the arrival of cinemas reading story books has become less popular?

I don't think so. Despite popularity of films, story books are widely read and good story books are always in demand. For example, J K Rowling's Harry Potter series. Since I am a teacher, I know how much teenagers love popular literature. Many times when I am teaching in a classroom, I find one or two students engrossed in reading Chetan Bhagat or J K Rowling. This is an undeniable proof of story book's popularity.

Q: 3 What are the things that make a good story?

Well, I am not an author but I think every reader expects some entertainment and some education from a story. If a story is predictable, a reader loses his interest in reading it further, while a twist in a story can make it more gripping and exciting. Nowadays, Indian soaps employ "a twist in the tale" formula to gain popularity, and they have really become popular.

Q: 4 What difference do you find between past stories and contemporary ones?

In past, stories were mainly based on some myths or historical event and they were written mainly to inculcate good values in readers but these days story writing has become just sheer business. Therefore contemporary stories are predominantly entertaining and less instructive. Besides, the changing values are also reflected in modern stories. For instance, contemporary tales overtly narrate extramarital affairs and surprisingly instead of criticising people appreciate them.

Q: 5 How does a person's age influence his taste in stories?

A person's age greatly influences his choice of stories. For example, children prefer to read some stories with supernatural elements or the stories in which a super human is shown as a hero. On the other hand, youngsters like romantic stories and adventure stories, whereas elderly people are more interested in spiritual stories or stories about their past. However, there are some tales that are popular among people of all ages and all nations.

Q: 6 What kinds of stories do you think will become popular in future?

Seeing that a modern story teller enjoys more freedom that a past story teller, I guess stories highlighting social issues and new technological inventions will become more popular in future. Besides, story-telling will not be limited to entertainment only but it will also become a means to educate future generation.

Interview 9

Part One:

1) What kind of weather is there in your country?

The weather in my country is generally hot from March to July and cold from December to February. In the north of my country there is virtually no humidity in summer but in its western parts summer days are hot and humid because there is sea nearby. And it rains in the country from May to August.

2) What part of a day do you like most? Why?

I like the evening most because in the evening I get off my workplace and can kick back at my home. Besides, the evening is the only time in a day when I can hang out with my friends.

3) What is your favourite festival? Why?

The festival that is my favourite is the Kite Flying festival or Uttarayan as it is called in Gujarati because during this festival friends get together and bask under the sun and enjoy flying kites.

Besides, there're many other things to enjoy like sweets, undhiyoo, which is a spicy vegetable dish and DJs.

4) What can we do to stop accidents during festivals?

During the Kite festival we should be careful while we are riding on a bike because a glass-coated thread may fall on us and slit our throat. We should be weary of threads hanging from electric wires as well. During Diwali, we should beware of fireworks by roads.

5) What do you think makes a festival memorable?

In my view, apart from eating and various rituals, it is company of friends that makes any festival memorable. I cannot imagine celebrating any festival alone without any friends.

6) Do you prefer to celebrate festivals at your home or at your friends' place? Why?

I prefer to celebrate festivals at my place because my house is big and most of my friends live near my house. However, some friends come from other cities but I put them up for some days. And since my friends love the food cooked by my mom, I like to spend some happy time with friends at my home.

Part Two:

An interesting letter you received.

Say...

When and where you received it...

Who sent it...

What it was all about...

What it was important to you...

Ans:

A few years ago, I stayed in a hostel as I was pursuing a master's degree at a residential university. During my stay in the hostel I made friends with Medhaj, a down-to-earth boy from a small village. We used to get along like a house on fire. Every morning we had tea and breakfast together; we went to university on the same bike and we accompanied each other for dinner. However, after I left the university campus, I did not hear from him much. And one day I got the news that he passed away. My pain knew no bounds then. I could not stop weeping. And all those sweet moments of selfless camaraderie flashed through my mind. And all the comforts of life seemed useless to me. Since I left the campus, the desire to meet him had been lingering in me. But his premature demise thwarted my desire. After a lapse of three years a letter was delivered to my home. I opened it and I was surprised and overwhelmed with joy to know that it was from Medhaj, the boy who was presumed dead. After reading the letter I realised that the news about his death was nothing but a prank played on me by a friend. Furthermore, I learnt that Medhaj was going to get engaged soon and he invited me to his ring ceremony. If this letter had not been delivered to me, my precious friend would have been shunted into dark oblivion. And I would have kept being foolishly contented without this friend. This letter has really rejuvenated our friendship.

Part Three:

Q: 1 Do you think that people will not write letters as faster means of communication are invented?

I differ from the popular belief. I think despite advancements in communication technology, letter writing will keep occupying a unique place in human society. Personally speaking, I don't find the same joy in reading an email that I find in reading a hand-written letter. For me, only the words written on a letter are not important but also how a person crosses his T's and dots his I's is significant, because it gives a letter personal touch. Besides, there are a lot government documents and legal documents that cannot be sent though emails. So letter writing, I think, will not become a history.

Q: 2 Do you think letters sometimes provide historical information?

Yes. For example, Jawaharlal Nehru's letters have historical importance as they give us an insight into his thinking and ideology. Besides, letters written by authors and poets also reveal some biographical information about them. Many times, such letters disclose famous people's personal lives, for example their affairs, which are not talked about in their books.

Q: 3 Do people nowadays write letters less frequently compared with past? Why?

I think at present people do not write letters very often as they have faster means of communication such as email, mobile texts, mobile calls and online chatting. Besides, a letter takes a good deal of time to reach the recipient. Therefore an urgent message cannot be conveyed on time if we write a letter. Besides, sometimes a letter gets lost during transit. That's why, at present letter writing has become rare.

Q: 4 What do you think is preferable for some confidential message—a letter or other means of communication? Why?

To convey a confidential message, I think, writing a letter is risky because somebody else may read a letter before it reaches a recipient and thus confidential information is disclosed. For a confidential message writing an email is better, I think. Because only the recipient has the password to his email so it is not likely that somebody else can get access to the confidential information. Besides, in email we can make some folders and save important data.

Q: 5 What determines the channel of communication we choose?

The channel of communication we choose is determined by several factors such as urgency of a message, distance between a sender and a receiver, contexts, authority and hierarchy. For example, if I want to convey an urgent message to my friend who lives in another country, I'll prefer the internet chatting, while a letter can be preferred for communication of not so urgent a message with a friend in another country. And obviously, if I am to say "hello" to my neighbour, I'll prefer face-to-face chat.

Q: 6 Despite the proliferation of communication technologies, real communication between two friends has become rare and more difficult. Do you agree?

Yes, I absolutely agree with you. There are several reasons for this. The chief among them, I think, is a hectic life style with a breathing space. Though everybody has a mobile with them, they cannot receive a call from their friends when they are at work. Sometimes because of difference of opinions and myopia, two friends cannot understand each other even though they are talking face-to-face. Communication is not just speaking and listening but it involves having something in common, which is implied by the Latin root "communicare".

<u>Interview 10</u>

Part One:

1) What kinds of friends do you like? Why?

I like friends that are down-to-earth and truthful because a down-to-earth person can be approached at any time and truthful friends can inform us of our shortcomings.

2) Why do you think we forget some friends and remember some?

I think we tend to forget the friends who do not stay in touch with us, whereas we never forget those whom we meet on and off.

3) How important are your childhood friends for you? Why?

My childhood friends are very much important for me as they are the people with whom I not only played and laughed but also cried. And it is easy to forget those with whom we've played and laughed but not those with whom we've wept.

4) What do you think are major threats to friendship?

In my view, major threats to friendship include selfishness, being totally occupied with our job and ego. If friendship goes sour, any of these reasons are responsible.

5) Talk about any conflict you've had with your friend.

The only conflict I've had with my friend was during my days at the hostel. I told my close friend to be my room partner but he thought that our camaraderie would make us waste time instead of study. And therefore, he refused to live with me and my feelings got hurt. However, later when I got the result of my final year, I realised his goodwill for me as well as himself.

6) How do you manage to stay in touch with the friends who live away from you?

In order to stay in touch with them, I write to them or chat with them on the net and occasionally phone them. Nonetheless, none of these can take the place of face-to-face meeting so I make a point of meeting them.

Part Two:

A three-day holiday you enjoyed.
Say...
Where and when you went...
With whom you went...
And how it turned out to be...

Ans:

I do not go on a long tour very often. However, during my student life I went to Diu and Somnath with some friends. It was not organised by the college but a few close friends of mine organised it. It was November of 2008, when we went there. And the weather was really pleasant as monsoon was over and winter was beginning to set in. First, my friend Bunty, Satyendra and I went to Asit's home in Junagadh. And from there we boarded a train to Veraval. It took us two hours and a half to reach Veraval. After reaching Veraval, we boarded a local taxi to Somnath. We caught a sight of fishing boats while we were in the taxi. Within an hour we reached Somnath. I was really enthralled by the very appearance of the roaring sea. It was half past five and we did not want to miss the sunset. So we hurried to a guest house and put our bags there and came out side. Then, we went to a nearby restaurant and had some tea and snacks. Then we strode to the sea-shore and stepped into the sea with gay abandon. We splashed through the salty water and took some snaps. We really enjoyed wading through cool water barefoot. The journey had worn us out. We wrote our names on the sand and photographed them before the wave had wiped them out. Then we sat on a sand dune and just contemplated the sun setting. The sun disappeared behind the sea and it started getting dark very soon. And the people in colourful clothes turned into dark silhouettes. The sun had set and the darkness enveloped us but we all friends sat there for an hour engrossed in listening to the song of the sea. Then we went to a restaurant, had dinner and went to the guest house to sleep. The next day we got headed for Diu. It was an hour's ride in a taxi to Diu. When we reached there it was ten in the morning so we had an ocean of time to spend there. We went to an exotic restaurant and savoured various delicacies. Then, we all friends went to a corner shaded by a big rock near the sea and guzzled a good amount of beer. Then, we hired a room in a local guesthouse and stayed there. Next morning, we got headed for home. The joy this tour has given me really defies any description. And a thought of it makes me very much nostalgic.

Part Three:

Q: 1 Do people tend to go on holiday more often these days than in past?

I guess in past people didn't have to work as hard as people do today, so in past people were not this mush tensed. Consequently, they went on holiday less frequently. On the other hand, at present, people have very stressful jobs, punishing deadlines and constant pressure to excel in their work. Needless to say they are rushed off their feet. All these factors force them to relieve their stress by going on holiday.

Q:2 What kind of holiday industries have come up in your country?

A good number of holiday industries have recently come up in my country. My town had only one holiday resort two years back but now there are seven posh resorts in total in the outskirts of my town. The new holiday resorts have all kinds of luxuries that holidaymakers can pamper themselves with. Besides, there are some tour operators who organise tours to exotic places, which, I reckon, is equally popular among local tourists as well as foreign tourists.

Q: 3 Do you think tourism is beneficial or harmful to a country?

I think to a great extent tourism is helpful to a country in numerous ways such as economically, culturally, socially as well as educationally. For example, by attracting a lot of foreign tourists a country can project itself as a most popular destination for foreign tourists, which can boost local economy as local businesses can get business from foreign tourists. Nonetheless, there are some prospective problems as well. For instance, foreign tourists, who are unaware of the local customs and ethos, may hurt the local people's feeling unwittingly, if they are not informed of the local customs and ethos. Apart from this, the place can get littered if they do not dump plastic bags and bottles into a dustbin.

Q: 4 How can a country attract more tourists?

There are a good number of ways to attract tourists. For example, a country can highlight its historical places, which may interest people of other countries. Besides, an aggressive advertisement campaign can be undertaken to draw tourists.

Q: 5 How do you think tourism can promote peace and cultural exchange between two countries?

Tourism, I reckon, plays a very vital role in making good relations between two countries. For instance, by visiting a country, we can get to know its culture and history, which helps us in understanding it better. Besides, during a tour there happens some valuable interaction between the people of two countries and it can lead to some important and positive decisions such as trade pact or educational initiatives. These things definitely improve relations between two countries.

Q: 6 How do you think learning about various countries can help us?

By knowing about different countries we can understand their culture better and explore business opportunities lying in various countries. Besides, we can keep abreast of recent advancements of science and technology outside our home country, which may be of great use to us if we want to have technological progress in our country. And last but not the least, understanding a foreign culture makes us more tolerant of cultural differences and promotes harmony among various countries.

Interview 11

Part One:

1) Describe the house you stay in.

The house I stay in is very simple. It has one floor only, which comprises a kitchen, a living hall and two bedrooms. There is a parking lot and yard too. As you enter the main gate of my house, you reach the yard outside the house and then the entrance of the house leads you to the living hall. At the right side of the living hall there is a kitchen and behind the kitchen there are stairs going to the top of the house. If you walk straight through the living hall past the kitchen, you'll reach one of the bedrooms. The other bedroom is just adjacent to this bedroom.

2) What things are peculiar about the houses in your locality?

The houses in the locality where I live have flat tops from which rainwater drains into underground water tanks. Besides most houses are built on high plinths because of water-logging.

3) What kinds of things do you think make a house more attractive?

There are many things that make a house attractive, for example its colour, design and surrounding. Besides, the interior of a house also makes it attractive. If a house is without any furniture, it looks very ugly.

4) In what kind of area do you think we should not build houses? Why?

In my opinion, we should not build houses in areas that are prone to water logging or earthquake or volcanic eruption, because living in this kinds of areas is very risky as a disaster can happen any time.

5) What kinds of things do you take into consideration before buying a house?

Before buying a house, I take into consideration many things like its locality, amenities available there, the culture of the locality, legal documents of the house, look of the house, what kind of materials have been used in it and frequency of public transport there.

6) What kinds of facilities do you think should be available in a commercial building?

In a commercial building, there should be drinking water, lavatories, fire extinguishers, a spacious parking lot, a lift and electricity available round the clock.

Part Two:

A hotel you stayed at.
Say...
What the hotel was called...
Where it is situated...

Why and when you went there...

Facilities provided by the hotel...

Ans:

I am a creative painter by profession. Therefore, very often I have to stay in a city where my art exhibition is held. Thus on and off I stay in a hotel. Once the exhibition of my paintings and sculptures was held at Contemporary Art Gallery in Ahmedabad. So for a couple of days I stayed in a very plush hotel called Lime Tree, which is situated near Law Garden. It was the first of December when I went there and it was pretty cold at night. The area surrounding the hotel had nothing special about it as it was situated by a very busy road. However, the interior of the hotel was very impressive both in its appearance and its services. Though its facade was rather simple and could not catch attention, the services provided by them were of high standard. For instance, the hotel butlers carried my baggage to the room I had booked and were always at my disposal throughout my stay in the hotel. Besides, the hotel provided me with a luxurious double-bed room with a wash room in it. The room also has other amenities such as a table lamp, a table, two chairs, a smooth tiled floor, a wardrobe, a dressing table and a small refrigerator. The bathroom was indescribably luxurious. There was a phone in the room for me to talk to the hotel management. I used the phone whenever I placed an order for meals, breakfast, tea or water. Apart from this, there was a lift operating round the clock. I really appreciated it as I do not like climbing up stairs. In addition, the hotel also offered cab services. Of course, they charged for the services. But, my stay in the hotel was really unforgettable.

Part Three:

Q: 1 What kind of care do you think a person should take when he is staying in a hotel?

While one is staying in a hotel, one has to be careful not to leave his luggage unattended as it may get stolen. Besides, before booking a room one ought to make sure whether the rent charged is commensurate with facilities and amenities provided by the hotel. And most importantly, one must know the check-out time of the hotel.

Q: 2 What are advantages and disadvantages of staying away from home for a long time?

There are a lot of advantages of staying away from home. For example, if a student stays in a hostel away from his home then he may become more self-reliant and learn to deal with any problem on his own. Besides, he may also develop a habit of spending money judiciously and saving some money for future. On the other hand staying away from family for a long time might make a person self-centred and in some cases detached from his family. Sometimes, if a person falls in a wrong company, he may go astray and become a ruffian, a criminal or a drug addict.

Q: 3 Do you think residential schools can be responsible for increasing generation gap? Why?

Though staying away from home makes one self-reliant and responsible, residential schools where children live away from their families cannot be held solely responsible for the increasing generation gap because there are some more influential factors for generation gap such as media explosion, youth empowerment, education, technologies and influence of other cultures. For instance, some elderly people still cannot reconcile themselves with their daughters-in-law dressed in jeans and t-shirts, whereas the young generation finds it simply innocuous to wear jeans and t-shirts.

Q: 4 A great number of people migrate from their home countries to some English speaking countries every year. What will happen if this continues?

In search of greener pastures, people migrate to English speaking countries in hordes. However, this trend can be gravely dangerous if it goes on for a long time because Anglophone countries will soon run short of means to sustain migrants coming from other countries. Besides, the countries from which migrants come will lose manpower and this can have serious repercussions on their economies. On the other hand, industries in Anglophone countries will not be able to offer employment to numerous redundant migrants and even their own citizens. And incidents of crimes may increase at an alarming rate.

Q: 5 It is said that those who migrate from their country to another country lose their identity. What is your view about this?

I think it is too sweeping a generalisation, which cannot be true in every situation and for everybody. To illustrate this, there are lots of Indians living in the US, the UK, Canada, Australia and New Zealand but they still celebrate Diwali, Navratri and some other Indian festivals, which obviously prove that they have remained Indian at heart though they are living in Anglophone countries. Nonetheless, I do admit that there are some youths who find themselves nowhere as they are the outcome of cultural and intellectual crossbreeding between two countries. But these people are exceptions.

Q: 6 Can losing one's own identity become dangerous?

Contrary to the popular conviction, I think if we want to bring about peace and harmony in the world, we must forget our own restricted identities and cultivate a magnanimous outlook to life. A Muslim is against a Hindu, a Hindu is against a Muslim and a Christian is against both of them. Why? Because all of them are mercilessly trying to fight for their religious identities. A black African person is humiliated because other fair skinned people think that their own identities are superior to other people's identities. Let's forget what colour we are, what country we are from, what religion we follow, what language we speak and what ideology we advocate and then peace will prevail.

Interview 12

Part One:

1) Talk about the lifestyle of the people of your country.

I come from India, which is well-known for unity in diversity. Therefore, I enjoy the privilege of getting exposure to various cultures and life styles. Every state in India has a particular life style. For example, in Gujarat people prefer to own their own business and most of Gujaratis have a sweet tooth. In southern part of my country people work in government or private sectors and rice is their staple food. Moreover, there are also some differences in their dressing styles.

2) What kind of food do you like?

Like most Guajaratis, i also have a sweet tooth. Besides, I enjoy eating spicy dishes like Samosa, Undhiyu, Khaman etc. Apart from these, I enjoy eating fruits and leafy vegetables. However, I abstain from oily food.

3) What kinds of clothes do you prefer?

I believe in simplicity and comfort, so I wear whatever I feel comfortable, for instance kurtas and pyjamas in summer and a woollen jacket and jeans in winter. However, I don't mind putting on special clothes if an occasion calls for it.

4) How do you adapt to a new culture?

By changing myself I adapt to a new culture. For example, if I live in such a community where vegetarian diet is not available, I don't mind eating fish or chicken. Besides, I'll also try to learn their language in order to mix with the people of the community.

5) What kind of life style do you like?

I worship creativity as a boon, so I like the lifestyle that celebrates creativity. For example, I'd love to lead a life of a creative writer or a painter or a story teller or a spiritual explorer. I believe that no matter where and with whom I live, my creativity should be tapped and appreciated duly.

6) What does creativity mean to you?

To me creativity is the ability to think outside the box. However, when one has some thinking that differs from that of the mainstream, one has to prove his stand and, I think, this is how one's creativity is tested. Besides, creativity is always connected with artistic expression, I guess.

Part Two:

Describe an organisation you know.
Say...
What the organisation is called...
How you first came to know about it...
What the organisation does...

Ans:

When I was studying in the University of Baroda, through a friend I came to know about Existence Foundation, which is a non-government organisation formed on the basis sheer philanthropy. The organisation runs various schemes for widows, orphans and people living below poverty line. Under the saving scheme run by the organisation, a widow can deposit hundred rupees every day and can withdraw the money with interest whenever she needs. Besides, the organisation provides widows with ample opportunities for self-employment. For example, widows make incense sticks, snacks, artefacts and cane chairs and embroider clothes and these things fetch them money. Similarly, the organisation also makes an ardent endeavour for welfare of orphans. A huge amount of money donated to the organisation is set aside for education of orphans. The organisation also runs a school for its children. Children do not have to pay for their education as the organisation receives generous funds for orphans' education. Apart from helping widows and orphans, people living under poverty line are also benefited by the altruistic work of the organisation since they get financial aid on occasions such as marriages or funeral. Moreover, the organisation also runs one dispensary for the poor.

Part Three:

Q: 1 What qualities are necessary for an organisation to succeed?

I think two most significant qualities an organisation should have are solidarity and affinity because it is said that united we stand. Besides, mutual understanding and sharing of the same feelings can boost the morale of all members of an organisation and can make them tolerant of each other's petty foibles. Besides, ability to work hard and co-ordination are also prerequisites for any successful organisation.

Q: 2 Are organised efforts always better?

Well, I see advantages as well as disadvantages of organised efforts. For instance, if I am heading a team of students for a cleanliness drive in my university campus, some students might work efficiently in cleaning the university campus, whereas some might shrink from picking up a broomstick. In this case, those who are shrinking from cleaning the campus, in fact, prove counterproductive. On the other hand when everybody in a group is aware of their individual responsibility and discharges it efficiently, it can surpass an individual effort. For example, while we are going on a tour, everybody shoulders some responsibilities assigned to them. Then, we can have a hassle-free and enjoyable tour.

Q: 3 Do organised efforts always work towards interests of the society at large?

Normally any organisation is formed on the basis of some shared interests and beliefs and so organised efforts are usually for betterment of a society in general. To illustrate this, banks, schools, colleges and railways are organised efforts for public interests. However, there are some exceptions as well. For example, terrorist attacks are results of well-organised efforts but they are against public interests. I hold the opinion that when organised efforts are made by some renegades, heretics or traitors, innocent people fall easy prey.

Q: 4 Why do you think people form organisations?

I am not sure but I guess people form organisations because in organisations their work becomes easy as there are many people to share various responsibilities and contribute to the successful completion of a given task. Besides, in team-work expertises of various people is tapped optimally and it is ensured that nobody is assigned with such a task that they are not good at. Thus, organised efforts increase the possibility of success. Apart from this, there are also some social reasons for organisations. For instance, a majority of a society is not ready to accept a particular set of beliefs or behaviour, then those who share these rare beliefs and behaviour will form an organisation and assert themselves collectively against the mainstream. Such an example is one strange group working for homosexual people.

Q: 5 Has it become easy nowadays to from a group or organisation?

Yes, I assume, it's become easier today to form an organisation than earlier. And media explosion is predominantly responsible for this. These days, anybody who is conversant with the internet and some social networking sites can form an organisation. Though such an organisation may seem to be nonexistent in its initial sates, later it can spread like wildfire.

Q: 6 What kind of organisations will be needed in future? Why?

Seeing that grey population is on the rise because of improving standards of life and advancements in medical sciences, in future we will need some organisations that actively work for welfare of elderly people and provide them with protection against unscrupulous cheats and criminals. Moreover, considering the harm we are doing to the environment, we will need an organisation that works exclusively for protection of the environment across the globe. However, such an organisation cannot be a result of one country's endeavours but a good number of countries have to be roped in.

Interview 13

Part One:

1) What kinds of occupations do people in your town have?

People of my town have various occupations such as farming, business, teaching jobs, banking jobs and some people do odd jobs. Moreover, there are some people who pursue their creativity as their profession like creative writing, painting, singing and dancing.

2) What kind of job can give you job satisfaction?

As I am an egghead, anything that involves detailed study, contemplation, research, reading, writing and teaching fascinates me and consequently gives me job satisfaction.

3) Do people in your town hop from one job to another very often? Why?

Yes, they do because when they start a new job, their level of morale is very high but since employers do not make any provision for any morale boosting activity, a kind of frustration engulfs employees, which compels them to hop from one job to another.

4) Why do you think people prefer to do a job in a foreign country?

I guess the reason for people's preference for a job in a foreign country could be a hefty pay and excellent work environment. In foreign countries, especially in European countries and the USA, being workaholic is appreciated and generously rewarded, whereas in my country slackers rule the roost in most organisations and government organisations in particular.

5) Do you want to have a job in any foreign country? Why?

If I get a teaching job in a foreign country that is safe to live in, I don't mind working there provided that I get a handsome salary. Moreover, there should be plenty of opportunities for professional development.

6) Do you prefer a job or your own business?

Though I see advantages and disadvantages in both of them, I prefer having my own business because in a business with a pool of talent and some investment, the sky is the limit.

Part Two:

Describe a historical place or a historical monument you have seen.
Say...
What it is and where it is situated...
When and with whom you saw it...
How you liked it...

Ans:

Anything related to history whets my curiosity, so I pay a visit to a historical place whenever I get an opportunity. One such historical place I happened to visit is Joravar Palace of the Nawab of Palanpur. The palace is a majestic edifice sprawling a vast area in the west of the town called Palanpur. Though this wonderful historical monument is situated in my home town, I had been oblivious of it till I was ten years old. One of my cousins took me to this place on one Sunday evening. There are two gates to the palace- the gate number one and the gate number two. We entered the palace through the gate number one, which is adjacent to the present head post office of Palanpur. I noticed that the thoroughfare of the palace was flanked by tall Ashoka trees casting their shadows on the thoroughfare. As we walked farther, we saw a very old building topped with a dome with intricate carving. From a watchman I learnt that his building used to be the Nawab's place for recreation. He used to come to this building to listen to music or make painting. Behind this building there is another building bigger than the building for recreation. This building is made of yellowish pink solid stones and is called Noorei- Jahan, which means the light of the world. Noorei-Jahan is the building where the royal family lived. It has eighty rooms of various sizes and each room has a balcony facing the big ground, which was used for a number of purposes such as sports, public gathering, public festivity and court hearing sometimes. The thing that commands our attention is the Mughal style of carving on cornices. As Islam forbids idolatry, there is no human figure in the carving but the carving abounds with creepers, leaves and flowers. The first guided tour in and around the palace rendered me awestruck. Its carving and impressive architecture has left an indelible impression on my mind.

Part Three:

Q: 1 How important are historical places?
Historical places, in my view, are of immense significance as they are silent songs of a country's saga, through which we can get better understanding of the respective country's culture, ethos, lifestyle and arts. Without historical places all countries would look alike with modern skyscrapers.

Q:2 Should entry into historical places be restricted? Why?
I am of the opinion that entry into historical places should not be restricted because if people are not allowed to see historical places they will not become aware of their country's rich cultural heritage. And if they are unaware of their country's cultural richness, they will go on missing something they have a right to know. However, some historical places requiring renovation must be out of bounds for visitors but after renovation is over, people must be allowed to visit it.

Q: 3 Should entry into historical places be free or charged?
I believe that entry into museums or historical places ought to be charged because maintaining such places needs some money and it is citizens' responsibility to preserve historical places intact. Besides, fees levied on a visitor will deter entry of those who simply come to historical places or museums to kill time. However, museums are not profit earning corporations so such fees should be nominal.

Q: 4 What can be done to protect historical places?
This kinds of places should be renovated whenever needed. Besides, some security personnel and curators ought to be appointed to guard historical places and guide visitors. Visitors must not be allowed to smoke or chew tobacco on a historical place's premises. Moreover, factories emitting gases mustn't be allowed near such places because gases emitted by them can spoil appearance of historical places. Some time back I read about Taj Mahal getting blackened by smoke emitted by nearby factories.

Q: 5 Can history be better understood by visiting historical places or reading books? Why?
Though nowadays books on history are written after a rigorous research and have pictures of some historical monuments, I firmly believe that only reading books doesn't make a study of

history complete. To know and understand history better one has to see historical places and interact with people who have witnessed important historical events. However, only visiting historical places is not enough either. In addition to a visit to a historical place, serious reading of some significant books on history is necessary for better understanding of history.

Q: 6 Do you think history is always written without any bias?

No, I don't think so. History is written by those who win battles and wars. Therefore, those who are defeated are always belittled and denounced. How can we get objective narration of history until and unless those who narrate history are unbiased in their narration? Many times history is reconstructed by information given by various people. This kind of information passes from person to person and some bias, opinions, preconceptions also get mixed with the information. As a result what we have is not objective narration of history.

Interview 14

Part one:

1) Do you prefer to eat the same or different kinds of food every day? Why?

I get fed up with the same kind of food very soon, so I prefer to eat various kinds of foods daily. Besides, eating various kinds of foods also ensures perfect nourishment as we get all kinds of minerals and vitamins from the varied types of foods.

2) How does your choice of food get influenced by seasons?

In winter I simply gorge myself upon some of my favourite delicacies, because in winter it's easy to digest food, whereas in summer fruit juice occupies an unrivalled place in my diet and I abstain from overeating as overeating makes me uneasy in hot days. And in monsoon my appetite goes down, so I don't eat much.

3) Are there some dishes that you don't like?

Yes, there are. For instance, I dislike Halvo, a kind of sweet delicacy typical of Gujarati food, because it is too sweet apart from being very heavy on oil. And I refrain from junk food as it makes us obese.

4) What kinds of restaurants do you like?

I like the types of restaurants that are in a state of art, that is to say, it should not serve only delicious food but also it should give pleasure being there. For example, there should be slow music going on, some beautiful paintings hanging on the walls and some other things that we enjoy looking at. Besides, going to such a restaurant should not burn a hole in our pocket.

5) Do you prefer going alone or with friends to a restaurant?

I'm not a loner but gregarious, so I can't imagine going to a restaurant alone. Friends' company, I think, adds some extra flavour to food. So I always take my friends with me to a restaurant. Nonetheless, if I'm alone at home and I have to eat food, I get food packed and carry it home and then eat it instead of eating alone in a restaurant.

6) Do you celebrate your birthday at home or in a hotel or restaurant? Why?

I celebrate it at my home because I get everything I need like music system, decoration of my room, photographing some happy moments and company of friends and relatives. And I don't feel at home in a restaurant.

Part Two:

Describe your visit to a place of religious importance.
Say...
What the place is and where it is located...
When and with whom you went there...
What you liked about it...

Ans:

Honestly speaking, I am not a very religious person and seldom go to a religious place. However, in the north of Gujarat, there is a small town named Ambaji, where an illustrious temple of a Hindu deity is situated. Ambaji is located approximately two hundred kilometres north of Ahmedabad, the commercial capital of Gujarat. When I went to this famous temple for the first time, I was accompanied by my uncle and his friends. From my uncle I got to know that the temple occupies a very significant place in Hindu mythology and Hindu scriptures. Scriptures say that when the Goddes Parvati immolated herself, her body was broken into pieces and a piece of her heart fell on a small hillock in Ambaji. There are two temples of the Goddess Amba in Ambaji- one is situated in the centre of the town and another in situated on a small hillock outside the town. As the temple is situated at a high altitude, there is a ropeway for pilgrims to reach the temple on the hillock. When one goes up the hillock through the ropeway, one can see the entire town from the passenger cabin. I like the place as it is surrounded by jungle and mountains. Besides, the nearby mountains are home to various wild animals and birds, bears being the major species among them. Moreover, there is a popular belief that if a person comes to the temple on foot on a full-moon night of the Hindu month called Bhadarva, the goddess Amba fulfils the person's wish. However, I do not subscribe to this belief but it draws a big crowd on that particular day. The serpentine ride up the mountain thrills me more than standing in a queue for hours before the temple.

Part Three:

Q: 1 Do you think religious places have lost their popularity among tourists? Why?
I think most of people prefer a beach or some exotic places to religious places. Therefore, we don't find as many people going to religious places as we did some years back. The reason may be that people go on a tour just for enjoyment and not with any serious purpose. Nonetheless, there are some places where we can see considerable rush of people round the year and hordes of people on some religious festivals.

Q: 2 Should religious places be given importance? Why?
I think they should be given importance because through them a person knows what faith means and what role religion plays in life. India is appreciated for its unity in its diversity. And various religions and religious places enrich India's diversity. Thus from cultural point of view, religious places should be given due significance.

Q: 3 How does a place become important for tourists?
There are many factors that make a place popular or important for tourists. A very common thing, in my view, that makes a place important for tourists is its historical significance and availability of amenities there. For example, Pavaghath is such a place that has all necessary amenities such as guest houses, hotels, restaurants etcetera for tourists. Besides being a religious place, it also has some historical importance. Thus it has become famous.

Q: 4 Do a great number of tourists visiting a place harm or benefit the place?
It has two sides like a coin. On one hand, tourists help local economy as they stay in hotels, eat there and buy lots of things from the place. Besides, local people also learn something about tourists' culture, language and countries. On the other hand, a lot of tourists also pose a threat to local ecological balance, if a place gets overcrowded with tourists. And sometimes tourists damage historical places and pollute local environment by dumping litter there. However, I hold

that a regulated flow of tourists can always prove to be beneficial to a place in many ways.

Q: 5 Do you think travelling has become less preferred a hobby since advent of the internet? Why?

Though easy availability of information by the internet may make us believe that travelling has been rivalled by the internet, the recent increase in domestic as well as international flights bears a testimony to the increasing popularity of travelling. There are many kinds of information that can be obtained by the internet. For example history and location of a place. However, if I want to know a place in a real sense, I've got to taste its culture and for this I have to travel to the place, see the place in person and interact with people there. Only words on a computer screen cannot give the feel of the place.

Q: 6 Should government grant subsidies for a journey to religious places?

It's a bit controversial question but I believe if such a subsidy for a pilgrimage promotes cultural richness and diversity without hurting sentiments of other religions, then there is nothing wrong in government giving financial assistance to people for a pilgrimage. Nonetheless, government has to see to it that such a subsidy should not become a coveted prerogative of one specific religion but a person following any religion should be able to get such subsidies.

Interview 15

Part one:

1) What makes you happy?

There are many things that make me happy but among all of them, the predominant is the freedom to be myself. I really enjoy being myself and the things that allow me to be myself are my close friends, my study room and my paintings and poems.

2) What kinds of experiences do think can teach a lot to us?

In my view, bad experiences can teach us what we should avoid doing, whereas good experiences prove to be impetus to self-development. Besides, exposure to heterogeneous cultures and life-styles can also teach us a lot of things.

3) What kinds of mistakes do you generally commit?

The mistakes I generally commit include forgetting names of people, forgetting important things to do, procrastinating when an instant decision is required and sometimes misjudging a person.

4) What do you learn from your mistakes?

I learn a good number of things such as sympathy, decision making and trusting people. My habit of forgetfulness has taught me to maintain important records in a file. Thus even though some information escapes my mind, a file is always handy.

5) Do you think experience makes us perfect?

I agree with this to some extent. For example, in a new job a person has to learn a lot, which is possible only through experience. However, sometimes experience makes us cunning and thick-skinned instead of perfect.

6) Do you agree that learning by doing is the best way of learning? Why?

I absolutely agree with it. If I just listen to some strange theories expatiated by a professor, I hardly understand it. However, if I experience something, I understand it better. For example, if I want to understand joy of creation, then I have to be creative. Perhaps I can make a painting or write a poem, and I can feel the joy of creation but only theories won't be able to make me understand the joy of creation.

Part Two:

Narrate a memorable event/occasion in your life.
Say...
What the event/occasion was...
When and where it happened...
Whether you can compare it with any other event/occasion in your life...

Ans:

It is said that life is full of a lot of events but it is not merely a series of events. However, I have come to know how strongly events influence our psyche. One event which I had eagerly hankered after and which fortunately took place is my engagement. I had been in a clandestine love with a girl named Nancy. Initially my love was unrequited as I was short of grit to wear my heart on my sleeve but then she turned out to be an acquaintance of my aunt, whom I requested to get me some information about her. And fortunately, it was revealed that Nancy was my caste and then with the help of my aunt, Nancy and I became close friends and as the relationship became stronger, we decided to get engaged and this idea of ours was embraced uninhibitedly by both the families. Consequently our engagement was arranged at my home on the twenty fourth of June last year. And a lot of friends and relatives attended the ring ceremony party. I still remember Nancy had donned a white gown and a diaphanous white bridal veil across her beautiful face. A typical Christian bridal dressing. And I was wearing a navy blue suit and a white shirt. I still believe that my engagement is a unique event in my life and cannot be compared with any other event because the ring ceremony, symbolic of marriage vows of fidelity and affinity, has given a new meaning to my life and made it more interesting. Nonetheless, I admit that there have been a number of auspicious events in my life such as my winning the first prize in the chess competition at the national level, my bagging a very lucrative job in a reputed IT company and the recent purchase of my own two-storeyed house in the posh area of the city but none of them can parallel my betrothal with Nancy.

Part Three:

Q: 1 Do you agree that past is important for a person? How?

Yes, I think past is very much important. If a person learns from his past mistakes, he can stop committing the same mistake a second time. Besides, past explains why the thing are the way they are now. In this regard, I'd like to give an example. While appointing a person for a job, an employer looks at his past. If a person has served in some reputed organisations, he is considered to be more efficient an employee and his chances of getting hired increase.

Q: 2 A single event in a person's past can be very decisive in his future. Do you agree?

Yes, I do. An event in past, however petty and trivial it may sound, has potential to influence a person's thinking and life to a great extent. For example, in my childhood my grandfather used to tell me stories and I very much enjoyed listening to his tales. Now, at this age I write poems and short stories, which can be attributed to my childhood passion for stories. Similarly, what career a person is going to have when he grows up is also determined by his childhood inclinations and what others think of his liking for a particular thing.

Q: 3 Can two countries have friendly relations after having a conflict? How?

It may sound difficult but it is certainly not impossible for two countries to have good relations after a conflict. In the process of peace making, two countries have to make a new start and forget past, forgive each other for their shortcomings and work for each other's betterment and welfare. What is more important in this is the ability to look at an issue from various angles, including that of the opposite country. However, if a good relation is just a feigned tolerance, an insurgency, betrayal or any other trouble can break out at any moment.

Q: 4 What kinds of incidents and events do you think we tend to remember? Why?

I think that we are more likely to remember happy times and favourable happenings as we already face a lot of problems in daily life. If I look back at my childhood, I can hardly recall any unhappy event. I can't remember when I was punished by my teacher but I do remember when and how I was rewarded for my paintings. Nonetheless, some people are pessimistic and are always obsessed with painful things in life. For this their attitude to life may be responsible.

Q: 5 Do you think nowadays people take less interest in studying history?

I don't think so. Seeing that other countries have begun to show keen interest in knowing about Indian cultural and its Yoga and we Indians also study American and British history in schools and colleges, it will be misleading to say that history has become less popular among modern people.Despite the decreasing number of students in university departments, people outside are eager to know past and history books prove to be best sellers. This is enough to make one realise how popular history is with people.

Q: 6 What kind of people do you think will be remembered in future? Why?

In future those who have invented some new technologies or written great literature or created master pieces of arts will be remembered. In short, trailblazers will be remembered in future because it is them to whom humanity is indebted for their contribution in various fields such as politics, literature, arts, architecture, technology, science and medicine. However, some notorious people such as terrorists and counterfeiters may also be remembered but not with reverence but with disgust.

Interview 16

Part One:

1) Do you live alone or with your family?
I live with my family.

2) How often do you meet your friends?
Almost every day. I teach in a college and all my colleagues and students are my friends

3) Do you like making friends from various places or the same place? Why?
I am a very sociable person so I can make friends with any kind of person, no matter where he or she comes from. However, I enjoy making friends with people of different places, as it exposes me to various cultures and thinking.

4) What kinds of things do you enjoy with your friends?
I enjoy watching films with friends, going out with friends and shopping with them. And I also enjoy playing pranks with friends.

5) Do you forget the friends who live in another country? Why?
I don't forget them rather I miss them a lot and am always desperate to meet them because when I think of them, happy time I spent with them comes to mind, which makes me want to meet them.

6) How do you support or help your friends?
I help my friends in their studies by giving them notes, in their tough time by being their shoulder to cry on and by counselling them when they are in a predicament.

Part Two:

Describe news about your family that gave you happiness.
Say...
When and how the news reached you...
What the news was...
Why it made you happy...

Ans:

It is said that no news is good news but I beg to differ from this popular belief because sometimes news can infuse us with a novel zest for life. Such a piece of news was conveyed to me by my brother during the first week of the last month. For two months he had been preparing to study in the UK when I got the news that he had been given the visa to the UK. I was just over the moon on receiving this news and a happy picture of my brother graduating from a premier British university popped up in my mind. In fact when I got this news, I was just plodding home after a tiring hectic day at my work place. But with a single beep of my mobile, the ennui and exhaustion disappeared suddenly. And my gait speeded up. Indeed, it was a piece of good news for me as my brother is the eldest among all siblings, his promising future can be of great help to all family members. And frankly speaking, I am also desirous of going to the UK for studies, so once my brother goes there, he can guide me properly as to how I can apply to various colleges and universities in the UK and how I can find fund for my studies. Moreover, I have been keenly interested in British culture, art and literature since my school days. So now that my brother is there in the UK, I can get all kinds of information from him about the things pertaining to British culture, art and literature. Besides, he can also air his opinion about the culture there and how it differs from or resembles mine. And I have requested him to pay a visit to the University of York where I would like to pursue my tertiary education. I am eagerly looking forward to some important information about this university that he is going to send me. After I am apprised of the student life, the courses offered by the university and cost of living in York, I will be able to make the final decision about my studies in the UK.

Part Three:

Q: 1 Why do you think a lot of people leave their countries and try to settle in other countries?

There may be various factors responsible for this trend. First, some threats or insurmountable problems like famine, terrorism, insurgencies etc in their home countries may be responsible for a mass exodus from one country to other country. This is true for many underdeveloped countries, whereas as far as developing countries are concerned, the pull factors are more responsible than push factors. Migration from developing countries to developed countries can be attributed to people's search for greener pastures.

Q: 2 What effects does migration have on people and their countries?

I think migration brings about cultural and intellectual exchange and thus enriches cultures of both countries. For instance, after migration to England, an Indian comes across and picks up English culture, while English people get exposed to Indian way of life and thinking. A host country is always indebted to its migrants for its cultural diversity. Besides, the country from where people migrate also gets influenced by this kind of migration, as those who have migrated get married in a foreign country and raise their children there and thus their home country's culture becomes totally strange to this kind of children.

Q: 3 Do you think that migration can also result in loss of skilled people?

Yes, I can see the possibility of brain-drain, if immigration becomes rampant. If those who are highly educated and professionally trained leave their country and settle in a developed country, it is a great loss to their home country. For example, if outstanding professors, scientists, doctors and authors migrate to a foreign country, people of their home country will be deprived of their services.

Q: 4 What do you think should be done to stop brain-drain?

A country can preserve its highly skilled and professionally trained people in a number of ways. First, this kind of people should be recognised and awarded for their excellence in their respective fields. Besides, a good number of lucrative jobs ought to be caused for highly skilled people. And last but not the least, if this kind of people want to pursue higher education, a collaboration can be made between universities of home countries and those on foreign countries.

Q: 5 Should other countries help one country in solving its problems? Why and how?

I think that if we want to stop the third world war, we have to learn to live together, which is possible only when each country co-operates other countries in solving their problems. Thus one country alone grappling with its own problems will become a passé and the entire world will become a global village living harmoniously. For this, numerous international organisations for a special cause can be formed. For example, to shoulder the responsibility of providing better education to people all countries can come up with one international organisation that exclusively focuses on education. Some contemporary problems such as terrorism and imbalance in ecology can be better solved by collective efforts.

Q: 6 If we learn to live together harmoniously, what kind of world do you see in coming ten years?

The very question evokes a rosy picture in my mind. I think if we live together harmoniously, all conflicts will be resolved and peace will prevail. Doors of one country will be open to other countries and intellectual and cultural exchanges will become more often and easier. Though there will be various religions and faiths in the world, no religion will be valued over others. The number of breaking families will decrease immediately. There will be more technologies for better life but no weapons of mass destruction. In short, the world will be a paradise in the real sense.

Interview 17

Part One:

1) What do you do during holidays?

I generally go to a library and read books of my choice or dabble in paintings or just hang out with my mates.

2) How do you make friends?

I don't do anything in particular to make friends but if I'm travelling by bus and a casual chat with a by-sitter shows me that my ideas chime in with his, we exchange mobile numbers and become friends. Besides, I also easily get along with my classmates and make friends with them.

3) When do you meet your friends?

There's no specific time earmarked for friends exclusively but whenever I am free or they are free, we meet and hang out. Besides, during festivals I certainly meet my friends.

4) What kinds of sports do your friends like? Why?

My friends like various sports such as hockey, volleyball, football and fencing but among them the most favourite is cricket because it gives good exercise to our body and it inculcates in us team spirit.

5) Do you tend to forget your childhood friends? Why?

Though I have plenty of friends at present, I'm still in touch with my childhood friends as with them my childhood comes alive and with my childhood come carefree days and feeling of nostalgia.

6) What did you look like in your childhood?

In my childhood, I had long hair, which was tied in a pony tail. I was very fair and chubby so people were attracted to me. Sometimes, my long hair also gave me an unkempt look.

Part Two:

Talk about a public holiday in your country.

Say...

What it is...

When it is...

Why and how it is observed...

Ans:

The life style in India sets a great store by holidays since people can relax themselves during holidays. There are many holidays here in India but I would like to talk about summer holidays. Because of sultry climate in India from April to June, a kind of lull prevails everywhere—in business, tourism, jobs as well as student-life. Therefore, students and teachers get summer holidays from May to June. In some educational institutes the summer holidays start in by the end of April. In the beginning of the summer holidays, railway stations and bus depots are found to be teeming with students and the people who are heading home. On the other hand, some people prefer this time for a rejuvenating tour. Thus it becomes pretty difficult to get a seat reserved in a train. Besides, during summer holidays flight fares also begin to soar high. Anyway, I prefer to spend my summer holidays at my hometown, which is a very small village located in a rural hinterland. I go to my farmhouse, sit on a swing under a shady tree and read good books or listen to music. When it is time for lunch, I cook food that is typical of a village life, and savour it to my heart's content. Then I catch some Z's on a cot. People go on a tour during the summer holiday but i do not. Instead of spending my evenings barging through a crowd in a street market, I would like to spend them sitting on a small hillock by the countryside and gazing at the sun sinking into the horizon. As the summer holiday is the period I have earmarked for rejuvenating myself, I spend a considerable amount of time with myself. Nonetheless, sometimes I go for a morning walk with my friends and of course there is scintillating conversation among us then.

Part Three:

Q: 1 What would life be like without holiday?

Terrible. I can't imagine my life without holiday because holiday is the only period when I can really recharge my batteries. I think life without holiday would be more like a monotonous song where there is no variation of pitch, neither any novelty in lyrics. Besides, we'd not be able to tell a Sunday from weekdays and we'd all look like robots programmed to perform certain daily chores and office duties .

Q: 2 Some companies give special holiday packages to the employees who have performed exceptionally well. Do you think this is good? Why?

Well, such a holiday package can prove to be an impetus for employees to work harder. Therefore, I don't see any negative effect in this kind of holiday package. A period of rest after arduous work rejuvenates a person and thus he regains energy and enthusiasm to work hard again. However, there should not be any kind of discrimination in awarding this kind of holiday package.

Q: 3 Do you think that the number of holiday-makers has risen recently? Why?

Yes, I think so. The falling airfares, increase in amenities for travellers, civic centres for travellers' help and a great curiosity to know other culture are all responsible for increase in the number of vacationers. Besides, compared to past, jobs have become more lucrative nowadays and industries are thriving. So people have spare time to see new places and abundant money to invest in a valuable experience of holiday.

Q: 4 Do you think people's preference for a holiday destination has changed over the span of time?

Yes, it has changed a lot. In past people rarely thought of vacationing at an exotic place. Instead, they simply chose a nearby place in order to save time and money. But at present, a person feels that his life is useless if he doesn't go on holiday to another country. Nowadays, the choice of destination for vacationing also depends on the purpose of vacation. A newly married couple would prefer some place rich with scenic beauty, whereas a politician prefers such a place where his privacy is not encroached upon.

Q: 5 What do you think influences a nation's choice of public holidays?

I guess a nation's customs, culture and history greatly sway its choice of public holiday. For example, in India we have a holiday on 26th January as it is our republic day, which is celebrated in a grand manner across the nation. On the other hand we have some holidays that have religious and cultural importance. For instance, Diwali, Holi, Eid, Rakshabandhan, Janmastmi etc. Moreover, in India each state has some festivals and holiday typical of its culture.

Q: 6 Should the number of public holidays be increased or decreased? Why?

Now that our life has become more hectic and we have been deprived of breathing space and are compelled to celebrate festivals and birthdays in an office cubical, an increase in the number of public holiday will prove to be a respite from busy schedules. Therefore, I'm of the opinion that the number of public holidays ought to be increased with a view to giving people time to rejuvenate themselves, as it's said in English "All work and no play makes Jack a dull boy."

Interview 18

Part One:

1) What kinds of co-curricular activities are done in schools in your country?

In schools here they conduct various kinds of co-curricular activities like debates, dramas, concerts, sports events, fashion shows, quizzes and celebration of various days.

2) What kinds of activities did you participate in during your school days?

In my school days, I took part in sports like cricket, volleyball and marathon, story writing, poetry recitation, elocution competition and painting.

3) What kinds of games or activities do you think can inculcate leadership in students?

If a student is given responsibilities of organising an activity like a tour, play, exhibition or any other activity, he can learn leadership. Besides, holding a rally also teaches students leadership, as a student has to get other people to do what he wants them to do.

4) What place do you think teaching of fine arts and performing arts occupies in an educational institute?

In India, it occupies a very crucial role as parents here want holistic development of their child and not only cognitive development. Performing arts and fine arts bring about aesthetic, affective and psychomotor development in students, so they are an inevitable part of any curricula.

5) What do you remember form your school days?

As I believe in living in present, I don't remember much of my school life except some happy moments when I was awarded a prize for my paintings or when I stood first in poetry or story writing competition.

6) Who was your favourite teacher in your school? Why?

My favourite teacher at my school was Mr Pradyuman Raval, who gave me not only knowledge but provided me with parental love, which is very much essential during childhood.

Part Two:

Talk about a contest you participated in.

Say...

What the contest was...

Where and when it was held...

What kind of preparation you had done for it and how you liked it...

Ans:

I still become nostalgic when I reminisce about my participation in a story writing contest at The Maharaja Sayajirao University of Baroda since it was the occasion that has boosted my confidence and morale. The story writing contest was held as a part of a larger programme called "Spark 2009", the university youth festival. Though the youth festival went on for more than a week, the story writing contest was held in the hall of Arts' Faculty building in the end of December 2009. As it was an instant story writing contest, I did not prepare any topic formally but I admit that my penchant for reading and my sensitivity to subtle nuances of the language proved to be an asset for me during the contest. Some of my class mates, who had been nominated for the contest and I entered the hall. And as soon as we took our seats, a senior professor announced some rules and regulations of the contest and after that he gave us a single topic "Dreaming About You", on which we were to write an original story. I was able to hear a lot of pens scraping against paper but there was a momentary silence on my bench as I was in a real quandary as to what plan was best among scores of plans crossing my mind. Nonetheless, I came down on one side ultimately and a continuous flow of thoughts began to come to mind. I was so much engrossed in the creative process of spinning yarns that I did not know when the final bell rang and when my story was completed. With the last word coming from my pen I felt a kind of deep satisfaction—satisfaction of not only academic progress but a kind of relief after catharsis of some ineffable feelings. The relief a mother feels after giving birth to a healthy child. I felt the joy of creation. Whether I was going to win a prize for my story was absolutely immaterial for me. However, I jumped for joy when I heard that my story had won a second prize.

Part Three:

Q: 1 Do contests teach us more proficiency or rivalry?

It's an interesting question. I'm of the opinion that if participants are aware of a real motive for a contest, which is to hone their skills by a healthy competition, then there is no possibility of a contest turning out to be an outrageous rivalry or fight. If a person participates in a contest with real sportsmanship, no negativity can creep into his mind.

Q: 2 Some people believe that beauty is to be appreciated and not to be judged and therefore beauty pageants are useless? What is your view?

I agree that beauty has to be appreciated and not to be judged so beauty pageants are not an infallible means to appreciate beauty. Notwithstanding, sometimes beauty pageants teach people how to appreciate beauty as they come across different concepts and expressions of beauty, which is in fact an abstract idea. In short, though I understand that beauty is not to be judged but to be appreciated, I don't consider beauty pageants entirely useless.

Q: 3 Should we hold various competitions and contests in educational institutions more frequently? Why?

I'm of the opinion that healthy competitions can teach a lot to students, so such kind of competitions should be held more frequently. Besides, some subjects that students find boring can also be taught by various kinds of contests. For example, a quiz contest can be used effectively in teaching of history. Though students may find it very boring to memorise numerous names of places, people and dates, their fervour to win a quiz contest can motivate them to remember all these things.

Q: 4 Do competitions and contests teach us better ways of socialisation?

Yes, I do believe that contests can also make us socialise better as we have to maintain decorum and certain norms during a contest or competition. Through a contest we learn to congratulate our opponent on his victory. Thus we develop a positive attitude in ourselves. Besides, if a contest involves teamwork, it can teach us better co-ordination. Moreover, those who are judges for a contest can also learn to look at the same thing from various viewpoints and consider opposite views as well.

Q: 5 Do you think that in future sports competitions will disappear because of video games and other indoor games?

As far as my opinion is concerned, no other type of entertainment can replace sports competitions, because they sharpen our mind and strengthen our physique. Indoor games and video games are popular but they do not exercise our body. Besides seeing that nowadays people's life style has become more sedentary, they need more physical exercise, for which sports competitions and outdoor games are suitable. And considering a growing number of sports enthusiasts, I don't see any possibility of sports competitions disappearing.

Q: 6 Can playing sports be dangerous? How?

Yes, I think playing sports like fencing, bike-racing, boxing, canoeing etc involve some risks and can cause lethal injuries if we are careless. However, on the other hand, I believe that everything can be dangerous. Going up stairs can be as dangerous as rugby, because if a person misses a step and tumbles down the stairs he may get some fatal injurious on the head and may lose life. Thus everything in life involves a possibility of death. But it does not mean that we should stop living. Similarly, we should not stop playing sports despite a lot of risks involved in them.

Interview 19

Part One:

1) What is your favourite part of your town? Why?

Though my town, being very small, has nothing special to offer for recreation, I like the campus of my college because with this campus are associated a myriad of sweet memories.

2) What kinds of places do you like to live in?

As I am an ardent lover of nature, I love to be surrounded by hills, greenery and ponds. Therefore, any place in the lap of nature can be my ideal place to live in.

3) What is your favourite city? Why?

Baroda is my favourite city as the culture there is intellectually charged and people there have an eye for arts and literature. It is my love for arts and literature that make it my favourite city.

4) Why do you like arts and literature?

I love them because they are the true voice of our culture and manifestation of man's understanding of the universe. Therefore they give us a unique identity.

5) Do you like modern art and literature? Why?

Though classical art and literature appeal to me, I also appreciate modern art and literature because they reflect contemporary issues and hint at our existential problem.

6) What kinds of books do you admire?

I hate potboilers but the books that have an enduring appeal fascinate me. For instance, some of the classics like “Tess of D'Urberville” and “Othello” as well as some of contemporary works like “The Alchemist” and “The Kite Runner”. However, I don't read self-improvement books as I believe that by reading books we can't improve ourselves.

Part Two:

Talk about a sports event you have seen.

Say...

What the games were/ game was...

Where and when it was held...

Who participated in it...

How it was...

Ans:

Honestly speaking, complicated rules of some games like cricket, volleyball, rugby and football are all Greek to me. And perhaps that is the reason why I don't participate in these games. However, I enjoy watching people playing these games. I remember one event when a sports day was celebrated in a school where I was teaching one year back. I don't remember the exact date but it was celebrated in the first week of December in 2010. From the morning till the evening the entire campus was teeming with students, parents and teachers. And surprisingly the students who frequently played truant also enthusiastically participated in a number of games on the sports day. The first game to be played was cricket, which interested all the people among audience. Some parents cheered their children, who were playing cricket. And some barracked the rival team also. Then, there was a game of basket ball followed by other games such as table tennis, badminton, tug-of-war, bicycling and a race. Though all the teachers were shying away from sports, it was compulsory for all of them to participate at least in one game. Therefore, I took park in tug-of-war, notwithstanding my reluctance for sports. There were ten members in my team and ten people in the opposite team. In the middle of the rope there was a red hanky tied to mark the middle point on the rope. I was at the middle of my team that is to say there were four people before me and five people after me. And as I am a bit underweight, I was literally crushed in the line of my team members. Nevertheless, I did not have to exert myself as my team members were really sturdy. Ultimately we won but at the moment of our victory we all fell over and I was crushed under the weight of three people of my team. I got some bruises but compared to the feeling of triumph I had, the bruises seemed absolutely non-existent. The event has dispelled the fear of sports in me. And I have begun to develop a healthy attitude towards all sports.

Part Three:

Q: 1 At present government is spending a lot of money on sports. Do you think it is justifiable?

I think the money spent on sport is justifiable as long as it inculcates sportsmanship in people.

However, there are many instances of some government officials appropriating the money earmarked for sports. If government money is spent on sports judiciously, it is beneficial. But sometimes sports events become just political stunts to gain people's favour, which, i think, is wrong.

Q: 2 How do today's sport differ from past sports?

In past, people used to hold sports event less frequently and such events were usually limited to their hometowns only. That's to say they didn't hold sports events across the nation. Besides, the sports people participated in were very simple. There were no shooting contests long back. On the other hand, at present some sports events draw participants from across the globe. For example, Olympic Games. Moreover, nowadays some sports like formula one race, which were not conceivable a century ago, have become more popular because of people's craze for new technologies. However, the sportsmanship has not changed.

Q: 3 Do you think there should be a particular time in the year for sports?

Normally sports can be enjoyed at any time, so there is no need to play sports at a particular time. However, I believe that in winter, which is very cold in Gujarat, people require more exercise and therefore this time of the year is preferred to other seasons such as monsoon or summer. And that's why Gujarat government organises Khel Kumbh, which is a state level sports event, in winter.

Q: 4 Should different countries have different sports?

I believe that variety is the spice of life. If all countries have the same sports, sports become boring. And a variety of sports lend a different identity to a country. Therefore, sports typical of a particular country should be promoted. However, in fact, in this age of globalisation, sports of one country can easily be learnt by another country. For example, Judo, which originated in Japan, has become popular in most of countries.

Q: 5 What role do sportsmen play in a country's future?

Sports play a very important role in a country's future as because of their ardent efforts and indefatigable sportsmanship a county wins a sports game. In short, they bring laurels to their country. Besides, they also become brand ambassadors of some products, which proves that they can also influence customers' buying behaviour.

Q: 6What sport or game do you think will become very popular and important on future? How?

I'm not a sports critic but I guess that football is going to be very much popular in future and will marginalize cricket in many countries because recently cricket has been blighted by many problems such as betting and match fixing. On the other hand, football enjoys unrivalled popularity in the US, a country which never plays cricket. Personally speaking, playing football gives us more exercise than playing cricket. Thus football will be a major sport in future.

Interview 20

Part One:

1) How do you get information about the latest happenings around you?

I get it through TV channels, news papers, magazines, books and grapevine sometimes.

2) What is your favourite TV channel? Why?

The TV channel I like most is MTV because it shows songs round the clock and I am a big devotee of music, whether it is classical, rock, pop or jazz.

3) What kinds of TV channels do you hate? Why?

I hate news channels very much because instead of presenting the truth to people they misguide people by sensationalising the presentation of news. And the reliability of whatever they show is often questionable.

4) What kinds of things do you discuss with your friends?

Though I am a laconic person, I do engage in scintillating conversations with my friends on and off. Generally I exchange with my friends views on various things such as literature, politics, arts, films and sometimes I also discuss with them future planning.

5) Who is your favourite friend? Why?

Among all of my friends, Asit is my favourite as he's down-to-earth and well-cultured. He also has the same hobbies that I have. For example, we both enjoy reading, site-seeing, painting and some quiet moments of contemplation. Besides, he is a shoulder for me to cry on.

6) What would you do if you succeeded in going abroad?

If I succeeded in going abroad, I'd study hard and earn a higher degree from the most coveted university there and come back to my home country to serve its people.

Part Two:

Describe a piece of furniture you have seen or you use.
Say...
What the furniture is...
Where it is...
What purpose it serves...
Whether any memory/incidents associated with it...

Ans:
Though I believe that the less one possesses the happier one is, I could not avoid getting my father to buy a study-table for myself. The study-table is very simple. Its frame is made of steel and on the top of it there is plywood covered with formica. It is in my studyroom in my home at present. It has played a pivotal role in developing in me a bent for reading and writing. My father bought it for me when I was studying in the ninth grade, because my studies entailed a lot of writing and extensive reading. Apart from encouraging me for studies, the study-table has also served another purpose in my life—that is as a memento of my father. Whenever, I look at the study-table, I am reminded of my deceased father. Anyway, I have seen my friends' study-tables, which are spick and span but mine is always a bit messy with a number of books and other things such as a belt, mobiles, mobile-chargers, a bottle of water and some polythene bags lying on it. And some scraps of paper in which I jot down some important things to do are always found on my study-table as a testimony to my weak memory. Despite its untidy appearance, I admit that I feel complacently happy when I cast a glance at my study-table topped with a heap of books, because it lends a scholarly look to my study room, and to some extent to my personality as well, though I am not a big scholar. Besides, there are some memories associated with the study-table. Fifteen years back my family used to live in a rented bungalow. And I used to do all my studies in one room adjacent to a big balcony overlooking the garden in the yard. My study-table was placed near the balcony and I enjoyed gazing aesthetically at the dangling branches of a big jasmine sapling bearing bunches of pink flowers. A gust of playful wind set the braches swinging. And my avid eyes were taking in all the beauteous scene, while my head lay cupped between my two palms resting on the study-table. Furthermore, I do remember some occasions when my study-table used be a platform for some scintillating conversations between me and my father.

Part Three:

Q: 1 What can be done to preserve our cultural heritage?

To preserve our cultural heritage, we should identify the buildings and monuments that require special care and renovate them without ruining their cultural beauty. If needed, such places can be made out of bounds for visitors and curators can be deployed to look after them. Besides, no gas emitting factories should be allowed in the vicinity of places of cultural heritage.

Q: 2 What role does furniture play in making a house comfortable?

A house without furniture, I believe, is a body without soul. I can't imagine living in a house without a wardrobe, a cupboard, a bed, some chairs and a study table. Furniture serves two major purposes. First, it makes a house habitable by providing some facilities to an inhabitant. Second, it enhances beauty of a house. One can live in a house without curtains but then the house will not look beautiful.

Q: 3 Has people's choice of furniture changed over the period?

Yes, very much. I remember that whenever I paid a visit to my grandfather's home, I saw some doll's house in a showcase in the living room, whereas this has become just a passé at present. Nowadays people don't prefer to have a showcase made in their houses. Besides, the old craze for wooden carving is also fading gradually. At present, simple looking furniture is in.

Q: 4 Do you think furniture will disappear altogether in future seeing that we don't have much space in a house?

I don't think so. We can't live without some necessary furniture such as a bed, tables, chair and a dining table since these things have become an inseparable part of modern life. However, I agree that in future houses will have less furniture or the furniture that can be folded in order to save space. But it is not possible for furniture to totally disappear from a house.

Q: 5 Are you against or for the use of plastic furniture?

Plastic furniture is sometimes more durable than that made of wood or steel because termites can do no harm to plastic. However, plastic is not biodegradable so it is detrimental to ecological balance and it stops rain water from seeping into the soil. Therefore I do not appreciate use of plastic furniture.

Q: 6 Does furniture differ from country to country?

Yes, it does. It also differs from state to state in an Indian context. For example, in Indian villages you'll not find dining tables because people take meals sitting cross-legged on the floor. On the other hand, in Indian cities almost every house has a dining table and a set of chairs. Similarly, the type of cots and beds will be different from country to country. I've seen luxurious beds with big canopies in some European houses, while pictures of Indian palaces show a different kind of beds. I think it is the unique style of furniture that lends a cultural identity to a country.

Interview 21

Part One:

1) What things do we need to be careful about in our home if there are children at home?

As children are not aware of danger involved in playing with some electronic things, we should keep this kind of things away from children. Besides, children tend to put things in their mouth, so we should ensure that there is nothing toxic around them.

2) Do you prefer a joint family or a nuclear family? Why?

I prefer a joint family as in a joint family our parents are with us during tough time. Besides, they can look after children, which strengthens the bond between children and their grandparents.

3) What things would you expect from your child? Why?

Honestly speaking, I'd not expect anything from my children, because I believe in giving them full rein. If they're given freedom, they'll be able to educate themselves. Thus education that comes by experience is far better than that which is imparted in a classroom in a formal setting.

4) What do you think we can learn from elderly people?

As elderly people are mature and have more experience of life than youngsters, young people can learn many things from them such as decision making, meaning and importance of tradition and social values.

5) What are the social values that you think are important? Why?

In my opinion, the social values that are important include respect towards elderly people, solidarity, fraternity, fidelity and tolerance because all these values bind us together in a form of coherent society.

6) Do you think social values differ from a country to country? How?

Not only from country to country, but they also differ from person to person. For instance,, in urban society punctuality and industry are more important, whereas in a rural society industry is appreciated but punctuality is not inculcated in people. Besides, considering the growing number of nuclear families in cities, it can be concluded that familial solidarity takes a backseat in urban culture.

Part Two:

Describe a toy you played with in your childhood.
Say...
What the toy was...
Who it was given by...
How you played it...
Any memories associated with it...

Ans:

There are a lot of toys that I used to play with during my childhood but among them the special one is a mouth organ given to me by my grandfather. Once I heard my grandfather's friend play a melodious tune on his mouth organ and immediately I took a fancy to a mouth organ. As I desperately wanted to get my own mouth organ, I wheedled my grandfather into buying one for me. And very soon I got my own mouth organ, which kept my entire house echoing with cacophonous sound, since I could not play any tune on it initially. Nonetheless, my grandfather's friend taught me some simple tunes, which I was able to play successfully on my mouth organ. Every morning I used to get up early just to spend more time practising playing the mouth organ. My days began and ended with music of the mouth organ, as I also used to spend a considerable amount of time practising on the mouth organ after dinner. However, in the beginning my friends from the neighbourhood looked askance at my new toy but then later they also started liking the music of the mouth organ. And a few of them were so much fascinated with this musical instrument that they forced their parents to buy a mouth organ for them. And they also started playing on their mouth organs. The mouth organ was not just another fad for me but it has influenced me in various ways. Besides, the mouth organ is still lying perfectly preserved in my house and its very sight invokes in me my childhood days full of gaiety, innocence and selfless camaraderie. When I look at it, I become nostalgic and desperate to re-live my childhood but a look at my present days devoid of any breathing space leaves a wistful smile on my face.

Part Three:

Q: 1 Nowadays children prefer electronic toys because of technological advancements? Is it a good sign for future? Why?

I consider this change as a positive sign because children's passion for electronic toys familiarises them with technologies at an early age, which later whets their interest in science and technologies. Thus, through children's preference for electronic toys, they get acquainted with science and technologies in their formative years. This early acquaintance later results into children's inclination towards serious study of science and technology. So I absolutely approve this trend.

Q: 2 Do you think the type of toys children play with have a great influence on their future?

Though I am not a trained psychologist, I surmise that children are greatly influenced by the type of toys they play with, since their mind is susceptible to influences from the outside world. For instance, a child who is obsessed with toy guns is more likely to become a soldier when he grows up. Similarly, preference for making houses by using compatible pieces or making sand castles is indicative of a potential architect.

Q: 3 Should children be allowed to play with toys at schools? Why?

I think they should be allowed to play with toys at schools since playing with toys not only inculcates them with intelligence and creativity but it also makes atmosphere of a school more conducive for learning. Besides, toys are not simply toys for children but they are the universe in miniature for children. What elders see as a doll's house is a potential household for children as it is through a doll's house that they learn how to perform their roles as a responsible citizen in a society. Thus, children must be allowed to play with toys at their schools because toys teach them a lot of things that classroom teaching can rarely teach.

Q: 4 Can we make learning a fun for children? How?

Yes, it is possible to make learning a great fun if a teacher is a resourceful professional. Though I'm not a teacher, on the basis of experience as a student I can say that learning can be made a great joy for children through an empirical approach of teaching. Instead of a teacher talking about some abstract ideas, students should be made to learn things by doing something. For example, instead of dictating an essay on rain, a teacher can take students outside and get them to splash about in the rain. Thus, students' first-hand experience of the rain will find a direct expression in their essays and essay teaching will not be tough time sharpening pencils and rubbing a rubber on a page.

Q: 5 What do you think can be done to keep up some games that modern children seem to have forgotten?

In order to keep up these kinds of games, we can encourage children to play them. However, we must remember that if children find such games interesting, they are likely to survive otherwise they'll be consigned to oblivion and however hard we try to revive them, they will never gain popularity. What we can do at the most is to arrange competitions for these games but we cannot coerce children to play them.

Q; 6 Do you think that those who play with toys can achieve more development than those who do not?

Well, it's a highly debatable question but I'm of the opinion that those who play with toys stand better chances of all-round development as playing with toys involves not only agility of body but also alertness of mind and co-ordination among team members becomes of prime import when a number of people play with a toy. On the other hand, those who've not played with toys pathetically lack agility and alertness of mind. One cannot become a good cricketer if one does not have these qualities.

Interview 22

Part One:

1) Do you work or are you a student?

I teach in a college. I'm not a student now.

2) What subjects do you teach in your college?

I teach English language, literature and business communication skills.

3) What do you enjoy most about your job? Why?

Being the master of myself is a thing I enjoy most in my job because I have full liberty to adopt the pedagogy I deem to be fit. And this bolsters my confidence and morale.

4) Do you like your colleagues? Why?

Initially I was not able to get on with them as their culture is very much different from mine but now that I've been teaching there for last six months I get on with everybody.

5) What is your ambition? What will you do to realise it?

I have an ambition to earn a doctorate degree from IIT and for that I'll gather some experience of teaching at a tertiary level and pass the entrance test conducted by I IT.

6) What are the benefits of holding a PhD?

A PhD holder has many prerogatives such as an exceptional command of his subject or discipline as well as expertise in guiding other research scholars of his discipline.

Part Two:

Describe a situation when you received important advice from others.
Say...
What the situation was...
Who advised you...
What you leant from it...

Ans:

It is said that advice is something that is given gratis and generously. Like other people, unsolicited advice does irritate me sometimes. However, there are some situations in our life when, being besieged by a lot of plights and predicaments, we lose our ability to make a right decision and this is the exact time when a piece of advice given by our well-wisher can save us from some misfortune. I also experienced some tough time when my vision got blurred and I was quite unable to decide what I should do. Fortunately, I got a good deal of advice from my friends when I consulted them about my problem. I was going to study at the University of Baroda, which is almost three hundred kilometres from my hometown where my family lives. The high quality of teaching and research at the University of Baroda was tempting me to leave my hometown and stay in Baroda for two years. On the other hand, I was also worried about my family as my father has passed away and being an elder son I was responsible for my mother and younger brother. Most of my friends from my hometown advised me not to go to Baroda and instead to pursue my further education from any open university so that I could live with my family, whereas most of my teachers and elders encouraged me to go to Baroda for higher education and improve my employability. Though the idea of earning a higher degree from a reputed university and bagging a lucrative job afterwards pleased me for a moment, I baulked at the very prospect of my mother and brother living without me. And the fact that I knew nobody in Baroda aggravated my worries. Nonetheless, I helped my brother in setting up his own business of stationery and when i saw him running his shop successfully and independently, all my worries eased.

Part Three:

Q: 1 Why do you think some people tend to give unwanted advice?

There're several reasons for it. I guess most of our friends and colleagues give us unwanted advice because they think that they're more intelligent than us and sometimes they give advice simply for the sheer joy of because they get a sense of superiority when they volunteer unwanted advice. However, advice given by elders, though it is unwanted, is for our good since their advice comes from their profound understanding of life and experiences.

Q: 2 What kinds of advice do you hate? Why?

I hate advice about what I should wear, what kinds of friends I should make, what subjects I should study at my tertiary level and most importantly what career I should make. I am of the opinion that one should have enough freedom to choose one's life. If I wear the clothes chosen by somebody else, I won't look myself. Similarly, if I study what others tell me to study, I'll be a degree holder without any concrete cause.

Q: 3 Do you think at present the generation gap has increased?

Yes, I think it has. Parents and sometimes teachers impose age-old ideas on youngsters, which youngsters do not like at all. On the other hand, youngsters go crazy under the name of fashion and freedom of speech, which makes elders uneasy. Thus generation gap comes about.

Q: 4 How do you think the generation gap can be dealt with?

In order to deal with the generation gap, we've got to make youngsters aware of and sensitive to their cultural heritage and similarly elderly people can be encouraged to be magnanimous enough to allow the youth their due freedom. In short, elderly people should not expect the youth to be their replicas and the youth should not hurt elderly people's feelings under the name of individuality.

Q: 5 What role do you think media plays in causing generation gap?

In my view, it plays a major role since young people are introduced to some unconventional ideologies through films, advertisements and popular literature. As a result, they get so much fascinated with these kinds of ideologies that they start following some bizarre things. For example, popular soaps show extramarital affairs to entertain people but people start behaving like characters of soaps in their real life. Thus media is responsible for generation gap.

Q: 6 How do you think the relationship between older generation and younger generation has changed?

Earlier elders enjoyed a kind of reverence from young people because elders have more experience of life, which has made them wiser than young people. Besides, elders were consulted in tough time or during any predicament or quandary. On the other hand, at present, young people have become more independent and do not like any unsolicited advice from their elders. Moreover, in the view of nuclear families, elderly people no longer occupy the important position that they had in past. It pains me to admit that the young people have grown careless to elderly people, though they're greatly indebted to them.

Interview 23

Part One:

1) What do you think makes a person perfect?

In my view a judicious balance of reason and passion brings about what we call success. Besides, there should not be an abyss of time between your decision and your action.

2) Who motivates you?

Normally nobody motivates me better than my desire to succeed does but sometimes I get motivated by the people who've acquired the qualities I've been hankering for.

3) Whom do you admire in your field? Why?

As I am an educator, there're many people in my field I admire more but the person I admire most is John Dewy, an American professor of psychology because he's recognised a child's ability to learn by himself and some negative effects that so called education causes on a child.

4) What age of people do you enjoy teaching? Why?

I enjoy teaching young people as they're innocent and open to new ideas, and they are very much impressionable. On the other hand, grown up people, say people who're twenty or more, have their ego, which does not allow them to learn.

5) What obstacles do you face in your profession?

In my profession, I face many obstacles such as absenteeism by students, lack of enough learning resources, hand-to-mouth salaries and stagnation. Besides, parents' apathy towards their child's education is also a big hurdle.

6) What qualities do you think are required in your profession?

In my profession, a teacher must have patience as some students are really slow in learning. Moreover, passion to keep abreast of the latest developments in your discipline is inevitable. If you don't have this passion, you'll lag behind and lose your foothold in the field.

Part Two:

Describe a trait of your personality that is special to you.

Says...

What the trait is...

How it is exhibited...

Whether it is helpful or harmful to you and others...

Ans:

Though there are a good number of traits typical of my personality and individuality, the trait my close friends believe to be predominant in me is my eloquence. Whenever I see something interesting or come across a crucial juncture of my life, some poetic words escape my lips spontaneously. For instance, I remember I was having a walk in Sayaji garden one spring morning and I knew it was my last morning-walk in the garden because I was going back to my hometown the following day. Two friends of mine were walking by me and contrary to my everyday joy and contentment, I sensed my imminent departure from my pals and the atmosphere of the city that revived a poet within me and some poetic words were uttered by me. Though I cannot recall the exact words, what I spoke was something like this. The garden that welcomed me every day with open arms has become alien to me. The trees whose cool shadows persuaded me to linger under them till yesterday have withdrawn their shadow today in a disapproval of my departure. The birds that sang my imagination in their songs have become silent today as if they have severed the fond bond between me and them. Moreover as a teacher, I am benefitted by my eloquence as it helps me in motivating my students and boosting their morale. For instance my utterance – "Every wave that rises on the ocean is destined to reach the shore."—has motivated my slow learners and they have made considerable progress in their studies as well as life. Besides, my gift of the gab has helped me in my professional as well as personal life. In my professional life, it has helped me to climb rungs of hierarchy and in my personal life it has strengthened my relationship and helped me to win confidence of my near and dear ones. Notwithstanding all these advantages, the gift of the gab also sometimes makes me ridiculous and bombastic to those who always fail to appreciate the beauty of subtle nuances of the language.

Part Three:

Q: 1 How important do you think a person's past is in moulding his personality?

In my views, a person's past greatly influences his personality. For examp e, if a person has always been ridiculed, he'll suffer from inferiority complex and as a result some dormant qualities in him will always remain dormant because he's never got conducive atmosphere for the dormant qualities to develop fully. On the other hand if a person has been give a full rein since his childhood, he's more likely to explore the things around him and embark on any adventure without reserve.

Q: 2 Do you think that films are mainly responsible for so many evils prevalent in the society?

I don't think so. Evils also existed when there were no films. For instance, Kauravas did not learn evils from any films. Besides, I think no evil can dominate a person unless he decides himself to succumb to evils. And films are not necessarily bad but they also inspire people to lead a moral life and fight evils. Moreover, films sometimes give vent to protest against corruption and thus help common people fight corruption.

Q: 3 What kinds of personality traits do you think make a person successful? Why?

I'm of the opinion that some personality traits such as honesty, candour, truthfulness, friendliness, adaptability, fortitude, magnanimity and sincerity make a person successful. If a person is a glib liar, he can initially win confidence of people but later his lies will get revealed and then afterwards nobody will be able to trust him any longer. Another trait namely candour makes us trustworthy and fortitude make us tough in tough times. When a person cultivates these traits, he becomes more successful, no matter whether he runs his own business or has a job.

Q: 4 What role do personal traits play in social relations?

In social relations much depends on personal traits as it is through our personal trait that we come to acquire a unique identity, through which people know us. If I'm not tolerant of difference of opinions, I will certainly fail to become a good friend and father, because there's is bound to be some difference of opinions between two friends or between a father and a son. Furthermore, a congenial nature works like a piece of magnate. That is to say it attracts lots of people and a good sense of humour works like lubricant. It makes everything go smoothly despite a lot of jerks and hard times.

Q: 5 What qualities are expected of a leader? Why?

I think that a good leader should have commendable decision making ability besides unrivalled popularity. During time of civil unrest, he should be able to resolve conflicts by his sagacity. In addition, good oratory, sharp logic, excellent ability to convince others and sensitivity to public ethos and culture are some of the prerequisites a good leader should be endowed with.

Q: 6 Do you think the people of your nation have changed much over the time?

Hummm..yes I think they've changed much specially over the last decade. The change can be seen in their outward appearance as well as in their attitudes to life. They've got more facilities to make their lives easy and sheer consumerism has begun to sweep through people as their job have become more lucrative and economy is booming. Moreover, there have been also some changes in the way they socialise. It seems to me that earlier an individual lived for a society but now society exists for an individual. Nonetheless, what has remained untouched by any change is the human nature. Though people have become more self-centred, during any calamity they stand together.

Interview 24

Part One:

1) How do people get to know about employment opportunities nowadays?

Nowadays people come across employment opportunities in the net, in newspapers and magazines. Besides, they also hear about employment opportunities through the grapevine.

2) What is your idea about an ideal job?

Actually I am not much hopeful about any job as I believe in having my own business, but in my opinion an ideal job should provide me with a plenty of opportunities for professional development and a decent pay.

3) What kinds of jobs do youngsters do these days?

Youngsters do various kinds of jobs like working in a call-centre, working as a data entry operator, working as a journalist and some youngsters also embark upon teaching career.

4) How did you get motivated to have the profession that you are engaged in now?

I was in the eighth grade when I first listened to my English teacher giving a talk on a poem by William Blake and the way wisdom kept flowing from him inspired me take up teaching career.

5) Who is your favourite poet? Why?

My favourite poet is Kahlil Gibran as his words have inspired millions of people, including me, to explore life with curious eyes of a child.

6) Do you think a good poet can become a good teacher? Why?

I don't think so as composing a poem and teaching a poem are altogether different tasks, each requiring a different set of abilities and skills.

Part Two:

Describe an important city of your country.
Say...
What and where it is...
What kind of climate there is...
What importance it has...

Ans:

My country has a good number of cities, which are important on account of their economy, cultural heritage, historical importance, education, geography or population. However, in my opinion, the city that is of prime import to my country is Mumbai, which was earlier known as Bombay. Mumbai, the capital of Maharastra, is located approximately three hundred kilometres south of Surat. Mumbai is a commercial capital of India, because a large number of leading corporations are located in Mumbai. Besides, a wide range of merchandise is made in Mumbai and exported to other states of the country. Most of the diamonds which are exported to other countries are polished here. The city is one of the metropolitan cities of India and is well connected with other major cities of India through railways, roads and airways. However, during deluge, the city gets cut off from other cities and consequently businesses in many parts of India get hampered as the merchandise produced in Mumbai cannot be transported out of Mumbai owing to water-logging. The climate in Mumbai is temperate as the Arabian Sea wards off chill in winter and keeps the city's climate humid and cool in summer. But rainy days cause some trouble. Furthermore, the city is also known for its cultural and historical heritage. There are many buildings such as Elphistone College, Mumbai University and Victoria terminus, which are typical of Victorian architecture and our heritage from the British raj in our country. Besides, the city is home to various communities such as Gujaratis, Marathis, Marwaris, Malayalis and others who follow various religions like Hinduism, Islam, Sikhism, Buddhism, and Christianity. Despite differences in their religions and languages, these communities have always lived in undisturbed harmony and thus made Mumbai a perfect epitome of the maxim—"unity in diversity."

Part Three:

Q: 1 Do you agree that cities nowadays are facing more problems than villages?

I think that problems are everywhere but where there are more people, there are more problems and cities are not exceptions. In my nation, which is a developing nation, there is a trend among people to migrate to cities for better prospects, which leads to several problems in urban areas such as over population, congested roads, illegal constructions, uneven distribution of wealth and rise in crime rates.

Q: 2 Do you think that life in villages is more peaceful than that in cities?

I am of the opinion that life is always peaceful no matter where we are. Whether we live in cities or villages we should be able to have peace. For those who want to earn more money and own their own business, living in cities may be peaceful as they get what they want. And when we get what we want, there is no tension within us and peace envelops us. Similarly, those who do not have ambitions, living in villages will offer peace as they will be able to manage with less expense.

Q: 3 How do you think we can stop people from rushing to cities from villages?

In my view, we should make all urban facilities and standards of living available in villages. For example, English medium schools and institutions of higher learning can be established in villages. Besides, villages ought to have some facilities like the internet, post offices, hospitals, shops, cottage industries and business opportunities. If these things are available in villages, people will not need to go to cities. Thus flow of people to cities can be checked.

Q: 4 Do you think life in metros have become tough or easy over the period of time?

I believe life in metros has become easier that earlier as there have been a lot of technological and scientific advancements, which have been exploited to make life easy and smooth. For example, in my city Ahmedabad, the local transport system has been revolutionised and it has become more convenient for people to travel by public transport than in their private cars. Consequently, such an innovation has eased the problem of traffic. Besides, if we want to buy something we have lots of options such as home delivery, the internet shopping etc. Furthermore, opportunities of employment have increased.

Q: 5 What kind of facilities do you think will be available in future?

I reckon that in future there will be a revolution in civic facilities. Seeing that there have been proliferation in places of recreation, I think, there will be more educative recreations and in order to whet people's interest in culture and history of a town or city, there will be some mobile libraries or mobile museums in addition to some information booths built at places of historical importance. And grey population may occupy an important place in future civic facilities.

Q: 6 What factors do you think make an important city?

Considering the present scenario of some Indian cities, I guess among all pull factors what is predominant is high living standards and safety. Off course, high standards of living involve better employment, booming economy, pollution-free atmosphere, availability of hospitals and educational institutions, communal harmony and excellent infrastructure. If a city has scads of employment opportunities but no communal harmony, then it will fail to attract people and as a result will not become an important city.

Interview 25

Part One:

1) What is your favourite destination for holiday?

Mount Abu is my favourite place for holidays as it abounds with natural beauty and in winter the temperature there is excitingly cold.

2) What do you carry with you when you go on holiday?

I carry several things such as shaving and bathing paraphernalia like shaving cream, soap, a towel, a comb, some pairs of fresh clothes and a brush. Besides, I also carry other necessary things like my mobile, my wallet and a blanket, if it is winter.

3) What do you learn by travelling to different places?

I learn a great number of things such as various lifestyles, knowing new places and savouring new variety of dishes.

4) Who accompanies you on holiday?

Normally my family accompanies me, if I'm not on a business tour. Sometimes, I go on holiday with friends only, as it gives me freedom to go wild.

5) What are dangers involved in going on holiday?

On holidays, there can be some dangers like accidents, theft, losing your way, adverse weather and mugging. However, with some precaution we can prevent all these mishaps.

6) When you are holiday, what kind of hotel do you prefer to stay at?

During my holiday, I prefer to stay in a hotel that provides neat and clean rooms at a reasonable rate. Besides, such a hotel should not be far away from the place I'm vising. However, when my family is not with me, I don't mind staying in a distant place.

Part Two:

Describe an accident you have witnessed.

Say...

When and where it happened...

How it happened...

How it could have been prevented...

Ans:

I would like to describe a harrowing accident I saw while I was walking back to my hostel. It was a Sunday evening and I was passing by the university girls' hostel. There is a sharp bend on the road that passes by the girls' hostel. I crossed the road and climbed the kerb and got on the pavement. Then out of the blue, a speeding rickshaw crammed with a lot of passengers popped up in front of me and whizzed past me. After a few seconds I heard a deafening bang. When I looked back, I saw a blood-curdling collision between the speeding rickshaw and a jeep. I caught a sight of a pair of eyeballs rolling down the road and some teeth strewn by the kerb. The very sight of a person's hair stuck on the radiator of the jeep sent a shudder down my spine. I was horrified but no word escaped my mouth. Then I gathered that these body parts belonged to the passengers of the rickshaw. Only one person among the eight passengers of the rickshaw survived the accident. The rest had a tragic end on the spot. However, the jeep has only three people and all of them survived the accident. However, they sustained some injuries and had bruises but these were negligible compared to the pathetic situation of the rickshaw passengers. The driver of the jeep got his leg broken while the rickshaw driver died immediately. As I was not looking at the direction of the accident when the collision occurred, I cannot say how it happened and who was culpable for this bloody accident. Nonetheless, I guess that the rickshaw driver was at fault since he was speeding, even though there was a sharp turn on the road. To cap it all, he did not even bother to blow his horn. And as there were eight passengers squeezed into the rickshaw, the rickshaw driver was not able to control the rickshaw. I think the accident could have been prevented if the rickshaw had not been jammed full of passengers and if it had slowed down at the bend on the road.

Part Three:

Q: 1 Do you think that the number of accidents have increased now? Why?

I hold that the number of accidents have gone up because of imbalance between population and availability of sufficient infrastructure. For example, in a city that is over-crowded, chances of accidents are high. Besides, people are not aware of traffic rules, which contributes to the increasing number of road mishaps. And attractive hoardings also distract our attention when we are riding on a bike or driving a car and we may ram into another vehicle or knock down a pedestrian.

Q: 2 What do you think can be reasons for accidents? How can we stop accidents?

There can be several reasons including reckless driving, ignorance of traffic rules, driving under the influence, bumpy or slippery roads, ramshackle vehicles, careless pedestrians and stray animals. In order to stop accidents, we should impose speed limits on vehicles, maintain roads and vehicles regularly, build sidewalks for pedestrians, avoid driving under the influence.

Q: 3 What can be done to spread traffic education?

For that we can do a lot of things. For instance, we can hold exhibition of paintings, perform dramas, conduct tests of driving and traffic regulations and arrange public speaking. Besides, various events relating to traffic education can be organised in educational institutions because they are the places where people come to learn.

Q: 4 What is the most preferred mode of public transport in your city? Why?

It is BRTS buses. As they're very spacious and comfortable even the upper-crust don't mind travelling by BRTS buses. Besides, their high frequency at most of the bus-stops has also attracted daily commuters such as employees and students. Some intelligentsia of the city prefer BRTS buses to their private vehicles because by travelling by BRTS buses, they can make contribution towards making the city pollution-free.

Q: 5 How do you think we can control the growing number of vehicles?

There are certain measures to curb the increasing number of vehicles. First, we should levy a heavy tax on whoever buys any vehicle. In some cities people have to show some solid reasons for buying a car, which deters people from buying cars unnecessarily. Further, if people have excellent public transport facilities, they'll see no point in using their own vehicles and consequently the number of purchases of private vehicles will drop.

Q: 6 To what extent do you think making some areas traffic-free areas can decrease the number of accidents?

I'm of the opinion that though we declare some areas of a town or city traffic-free areas, there are bound to happen some road mishaps on highways and other areas that are not traffic-free areas. However, I also agree to some extent that declaring some areas traffic-free can definitely reduce the number of accidents, especially in central parts of a city.

IMPORTANT NOTE

- Interviews 26 to 50 have the language bit simpler than the language used in interviews 1 to 25.

- Students educated in non-English medium schools will find them very interesting.

- Others will appreciate ideas expressed and pertinent use of cohesive devises.

- The vocabulary used in these interviews is not so difficult but rather it is simple and effective.

- You can learn the one great thing from this segment and it is how to make an effective use of your knowledge resources.

Interview 26

Part One:

1) How well do you know the people who live next door to you?
Sir, it is very difficult to know all the people living next to my house. But I can say for certain that all the people living on both the sides of my house are very good and co operative. As my father works in a banking sector, he keeps getting transferred every three years so we get new neighbours every three years which makes it tough for me to know my neighbours well.

2) How often do you see them? (why/why not?)
We have the habit of going for a stroll every evening after dinner so we normally see all my neighbours every day. But during weekend, we usually sit together for gossiping in the common area of our society. As the person living on the right hand of my house does a marketing job, I don't get a chance to see him often as he is mostly on tour.

3) What kinds of problems do people sometimes have with their neighbours?
I am quite lucky in that regard but normally people do have problems with their neighbours. Usually the roots of the problems are never so serious. Difference of opinions in the matters concerning both, conflicts sharing the common space, allegations of not being reciprocal in help and support are some of the reasons why neighbours have problems with each other.

4) How do you think neighbours can help each other?
It is correctly said that neighbours are the first relatives. Especially during emergency and accidents, it is the moral responsibility of any good neighbour to reach out to his or her neighbour. During social events, a neighbour should extend the helping hand. I believe that it will be all right if a person cannot help the neighbour in good times but he or she should certainly be there to help in adverse times.

Part Two:

Describe a time when you were asked to give your opinion in a questionnaire or a survey
Say:
What the questionnaire/survey was about...
Why you were asked to give your opinions...
What opinions you gave and explain how you felt about giving your opinions in this questionnaire/survey...

Ans:
Thanks...
I faced a questionnaire when I was pursuing my graduation. It was a survey being conducted by a well known magazine called ABHIYAN. The topic of the survey was about the recent surge in the number of Indian students migrating abroad for further education despite having good

educational institutions in the home country. I was asked three questions. First I was asked what I thought were the main reasons for this trend. I replied that good opportunities available in foreign land and poor infrastructure in the education sector in the home country are two main reasons. I also emphasised that there are students, though very few who just go abroad in search of instant money and job. Then I was asked whether it was a negative or positive change. Let me admit here that I was in utter confusion in giving a reply to this question. I simply said that given the trend of globalisation, any change will have both the impacts on the country but personally I don't find this trend negative. Then I was asked whether I was considering going abroad. I replied in a rather diplomatic manner. I said, 'I am not in a position to say anything at the moment as I can not make this decision myself without taking my family members into confidence. But the option is always open.'

First time I felt how difficult it is to frame our individual opinions as far as issues concerning general interests are concerned. It was the first time I faced any public media in my life. I experienced on that day that being a part of such studies and surveys truly shapes and influences our belief system. It broadens our mental horizons as we get to know many more viewpoints on the same issue. It sometimes makes us doubt our own beliefs. But I believe, that experience made me more critical in my thinking. I learnt to frame opinions slowly but firmly.

Part Three:

Q.1 What kinds of organisations want to find out about people's opinions?

Knowing people's opinion is very significant for doing any work of public good and welfare. Social organisations and NGOs are more concerned regarding people's opinion as it is the only source for them to determine the future course of any action. Political parties and government agencies also conduct timely surveys of people to know their views in context of national issues. It helps them make better policies and even to get innovative ideas from civil society. Media houses both print and electronic also undertake the studies to predict election results and to know the reactions of people to public events.

Q.2 Do you think that questionnaires or surveys are good ways of finding out people's opinions?

To a major extent, it is a very effective way of reaching out to people personally and extracting their opinions. The most important aspect of it is that questionnaires give ample chance to people to leisurely express their views. It is normally observed that views expressed in the surveys are more reliable than views expressed through any other medium. Opinion polls during elections are the best example of this. Genuinely conducted opinion polls are more or less similar to the actual election results.

Q.3 What reasons might people have for not wanting to give their opinions?

Reasons vary from person to person. But generally speaking, the reason why people generally avoid making their opinion public is that they hold the view that it is completely their prerogative whether to speak or not. They believe that privately held opinions should not be made public. However the same people willingly give the opinions on the condition of anonymity. Celebrities avoid answering in order to avert any kind of controversy. Some people are afraid to speak publicly as they might have opinions which they view to be publicly unacceptable. Apart from these, I don't see any reason why people should not speak up.

Q.4 Do you think it would be a good idea for schools to ask students their opinions about lessons?

It has both the sides. Being immature, students can not be expected to give impartial and unbiased opinions. Hence the outcome of the survey will not be reliable. Students will look at their side of comfort and ease. Looking from the opposite point of view, such surveys will help us know their reactions in regard to their lessons. It will help teachers to know the effectiveness of the lessons given. Feedback of students is the best source to know whether the given lessons are good or bad

Q.5 What would the advantages for schools be if they asked students their opinions?

It will help the educators to evaluate their educational policies. Knowing the likes and dislikes of students is very important for school authorities and educators to teach students in the effective manner. And such surveys are the best tool to do so. But again the question is whether students will express impartial and unbiased opinions or not.

Q.6 Would there be any disadvantages in asking students'opinions?

First of all, it is very difficult to ascertain whether the opinions given are true and authentic as students are immature at the age of study. Students are likely to imitate their friends or peers. If majority of the opinions of students are not in tune with existing norms of the school, it will create much confusion for the school authorities.

Interview 27

Part One:

1) Do you like to have flowers in your home?[why/whynot?]

Flowers are one of the most beautiful creations of nature. Having them at home embellishes the beauty of one's home. Flowers make our day. I certainly like to have flowers at my home as flowers make us feel closer to nature. Since my house is very congested with furniture, it lacks the touch of originality. Apart from this, watching fresh flowers in the early morning soothes our eyes.

2) Where would you go to buy flowers?[why?]

We have an exclusive flower market in our town where you will find so many florists sitting across the lines of the road selling fresh flowers in the morning. In my case, I am lucky as there is a flower shop close to my home where one can avail fresh flowers throughout the day.

3) On what occasions would you give someone flowers?

Flowers stand for delicacy and beauty. I think every occasion can be graced with flowers. Even during funerals, floral tribute is given to the departed soul. Normally, I prefer giving flowers on the happy and auspicious occasions like birthdays, wedding anniversaries, ring ceremonies etc. I also like to offer flowers to wish the person on the day which is special to him like exams, competitions, sports etc. Exchange of flowers occasionally among the near and dear ones stands for respect to relations.

4) Are flowers important in your culture?[why/why not?]

Flowers are so interwoven in our culture that any culture event will remain incomplete without them. No religious or cultural ceremony can take place without them. Flowers stand for beauty and gracefulness. Right from worshipping God to greeting any human, from birth days to offering condolences to the deceased one, flowers are very significant.

Part Two:

Describe a meeting you remember going to at work, college or school.
Say...
When and where the meeting was held...
Who was at the meeting...
What the people at the meeting talked about and explain why you remember going to this meeting.

Ans:

Either in the student life or in the professional life, one has to attend meetings. Here I remember the meeting I attended during my college days. I was in the last year of my graduation. The meeting was held in the conference room of my college. It was attended by the principal, other six professors and ten representatives from students. I enjoyed the status of being one of the representatives of more than three hundred students. The meeting was about organizing the farewell function of the students of the last year. It was decided in the meeting that the function would be followed by a nice cultural programme which would be choreographed and played by the students themselves.

Everybody was asked how to make the function a memorable one. Everybody offered his or her inputs. The principal explained importance of the function and made us aware of the fact why this programme held a great significance since it was happening first time in the history of our college. A special committee was formed consisting five students who had the interest and experience of organising such events. I was fortunate enough to have been the part of that decision making committee. We were given absolutely free hand in deciding what kinds of programmes should be played, who the performers would be, what the timing would be etc. The main reason why it was special for me is that my all my suggestions were agreed upon by all hands. I was unanimously made an incharge of the function. Above all, it was my suggestion to mark the farewell function with the cultural function. The principal not only accepted my inputs with open arms but appreciated them whole heartedly. It was the first formal meeting of my life and I had a nice experience with it. The first round of the meeting ended conclusively. Though that meeting was accompanied with other few meeting and we came to the final blueprint of the programme.

Part Three:

Q.1 What are the different types of meetings that people often go to?

Everybody has to attend a meeting in the life. Normally people go to attend the meetings which are social and professional in nature. By and large, we attend the meeting if we are members of any organisation or club. Whenever any big decision concerning many people's interest has to be made, it can not be made single headedly or autocratically, All the concerning people have to be consulted. With this logic, one has to remain present in many meetings as every person is directly or indirectly connected with various bodies of society.

Q.2 Some people say that no-one likes to go to meetings-What do you think?

Absolutely, many people simply hate attending meetings. There are various reasons for this public behaviour. When a meeting is of their dislike or it has to be compulsorily attended, it doesn't generate much interest. Parliamentarians dozing off in the parliament are the best example of this. Another thing is that when meetings take place regularly as per the norms of a company or an organization without any agenda, concerned people attend it for the sake of attending. Meetings of all sorts are bound to remain bit less interesting as they are formal in nature. As willingly or unwillingly, one has to abide by the protocol, it allows little freedom. But in some cases, people are so excited about attending meet if the subject matter of a meeting appeals to them.

Q.3 Why can it sometimes be important to go to a meeting?

Attending meeting is most important whether one likes or not. Failing to turn up for meetings may result into our getting bad image if we are the member of any organization or an employee of a company. A person gets thrown out of the mainstream and can not keep up with the regular occurring if he or she doesn't attend any meeting. A person may lag far behind in the ladder of knowledge.

Q.4 Why do you think world leaders often have meetings together?

World leaders often have meetings together as it is very important in easing the international tension. Dialogues and discussions are the only two weapons which can solve even the most puzzling questions of the world. Apart from this, it is a proven fact in modern global environment that no country can prosper if it overlooks the rest of the world. Establishing trade links, sports links and links of transportation is of paramount importance for any country to prosper. This is possible only by political dialogues. That's why we often hear the words like “bilateral and unilateral relations” in newspaper and television. International meetings by the world leaders are always for the good and betterment.

Q.5 What possible difficulties might be involved in organizing meetings between world leaders?

The major stumbling block would be to finalize the venue which should be agreeable to all the participating countries. . If the decided venue is not approved by the any country which doesn't enjoy good relation with the host country, the concerned country might skip the meeting. In such politically charged and sensitive discussions where world's top leaders gather at the same places it is very difficult for the host country to arrange the strictest security measures in place. To ensure the equal representation of all the nations is also the main issue.

Q.6 Do you think that meetings between international leaders will become more frequent in the future? Or will there be less need for world leaders to meet?
I personally believe that the frequency will increase in the upcoming future. Video conferencing and virtual meetings can never replace the real meetings. The new world has raised some serious issues affecting the global community. In the changing world dominated by technology, no problem has truly remained area-specific or a nation-specific. Problems are also getting universalised. In order to solve them, a dialogue is the only solution. Close observation of the history also reveals that the frequency of such meets has been increasing. Every nation nowadays agrees to the fact that violence and war can only add to the existing woes. Only through dialogues and discussions, issues can be sorted out. All these facts lead me to state that such meets will be more in coming times.

Interview 28

Part One:

1)How do you usually contact your friends? [Why?]
Talking about my close friends, I prefer meeting them personally. Being a person of a gregarious nature, I have large group of friends. Frankly admitting, it is next to impossible to meet each one personally. But thanks to the technology, I can occasionally call them by mobile. I even text them the messages of good essence. The best medium is the use of social networking sites. I am a regular user of 'facebook' and 'twitter'. I can update my latest moments and even get instant reply. I am basically an extrovert personality. I love sharing all of my feelings with my friends. And perhaps that is the reason why I always prefer to remain in regular touch with all of my friends.

2) Do you prefer to contact different people in different ways?[Why?]
I do prefer so and it is important too. You cannot contact all the people in the same fashion. I love personally calling on all the people with whom I share extremely close relations. For acquaintances, I prefer updating the information on social networking sites or sometimes texting them through mobile. As far as elders and respectable people are concerned, I always go and humbly meet them personally. It is up to the person whom I am supposed to meet and contact that I decide the mode of contact.

3) Do you find it easy to keep in contact with friends and family?[why or why not?]
Obviously it is not so difficult. On the contrary, I find it extremely easy to keep in touch with friends and family. In the world of highly advanced electronic gadgets, I never find myself far from them, however far I might be from them physically. Regularly sending text messages,

frequently calling, surfing social networking sites are some of the ways which never let us feel far from our near and dear ones. Technology has truly reduced geographical distance and physical boundaries.

4) In your country did people in the past keep in contact in the same way as they do today?[why or why not?]

No, absolutely not. Actually there are lots of differences in the ways people used to keep contact in the past and they do today. The only way of keeping contact available was either sending envelops or telephoning. The frequency of making contacts was also very less. Nowadays, people make use of electronic gadgets to keep in touch with their friends and relatives. The frequency of making contacts has also increased a lot as the communication process today has become quite cheaper and faster as well.

Part Two:

Describe a party that you enjoyed.

Say...

Whose party it was and what it was celebrating...

Where the party was held and who went to it...

What people did during the party and explain what you enjoyed about this prty...

Ans:

I here would like to recollect one of the most beautiful memories of the birth day celebrations of my friend Vaishali. The party was held at her own house which is at the stone's throw from my home. The party held the special significance for me because I was given the responsibility of organising it and ensuring that it ends successfully. Almost all the friends were invited and her relatives too were present there. For me the party proved to be the best place for all the common friends to come together and have some pleasurable moments. All the friends were completely engrossed in gossiping as it was after a pretty long time that they had come together. The atmosphere was charged with lot of joy and fun. Everybody's face was radiating lot of energy and charm. Vaishali was inundated with lot of gifts by her friends and relatives.

The main source of attraction for all was the most eye catching decoration. The room was completely covered by colourful balloons. We had ordered the big piece of 3 k.g. cake with the pet name of Vaishali i.e. TINY written on the cake. People wished her a lot on the day. Elders showered their blessings on her. She turned bit emotional after seeing lot of affections and emotions being showered upon her. People had a nice dinner over there. All the items were of my choice and they were appreciated too. It was a wonderful scene to see so many gifts being exchanged on that day. Since I was given a key role of ensuring that the party ends successfully, I didn't get enough time to mingle with friends and have fun with them. Despite this, I enjoyed it as it was the first occasion of my life which was solely organised by me and that too successfully. I was bit nervous initially but as the party progressed further, I started getting relieved. It was really the most helpful experience of my life. That experience has truly helped me in organising many functions in my life.

Part Three:

Q.1 What are the main reasons why people organise family parties in your country?
The main reason why people organise family parties is that nowadays people lead hectic life and they are not in the position to spare quality time for their family members. Parties are the best medium, according to them, to have some good time with one's family members. Another reason is that such parties provide welcome change. They are truly refreshing. Family celebrations offer a nice break from the monotonous lifestyle. One reason which cannot be denied is that it has become a fashion symbol. The influence of party culture from the western society does contribute to this trend. Many people simply organise parties for the sake of it without feeling actual need of it.

Q.2 In some places people spend a lot of money on parties that celebrate special family events. Is this ever true in your country? Do you think this is a good trend or a bad trend?
Yes, spending money in astronomical figures is not uncommon in our countries. Since the spending power of people is rising day by day, such extravagant expenditure for family celebrations has come in vogue. It is very difficult to use any adjective like 'good' or 'bad' forsuch events. From individual's point of view, there is nothing wrong in it as an individual has the complete right over the money he or she possesses. Nobody can dictate them. It also helps in circulating money in the nation. But I think any socially sensitive person will think twice before indulging in such extravaganzas. There are many better ways to celebrate family functions and the saved amount can instead be utilised for constructive purposes.

Q.3 Are there many differences between family parties and parties given by friends? Why do you think this is?
In family parties, there is a protocol one has to follow. There is always a limitation on behaviour as there is always a presence of elders. Family parties are always for a cause. In family parties, one has to perform certain responsibilities of arranging the party and welcoming guests. It mars the joy and pleasure sometimes. Parties offered by friends are bound to be more pleasant and joyous than family parties. Since all the people in the party are of the same age, the environment is always free and frank. As we don't have responsibilities, we can enjoy it better.

Q.4 What kinds of national celebration do you have in your country?
We have two main celebrations in the forms of an independence day and a republic day. There are certain others as well but these two hold the most significance in our national life. People of all age groups and of all communities whole heartedly participate in the celebration of these two national events. An army parade is carried out in the national capital. The prime minister and chief ministers of respective states address the nation. The entire nation gets emotional remembering the sacrifices made to achieve political freedom. We can see the waves of patriotism across the nation.

Q.5 Who tends to enjoy national celebrations more: young people or old? Why?
I personally believe that every person has deep rooted attachment with his or her motherland.

Age can never be a barrier in expressing that affection towards one's nation. But one thing is for sure that young people can participate in those celebrations more passionately. Elders too can extend their helping hand in organising such national celebrations. I think people of all age groups and of all the diverse backgrounds tend to get enjoyment to their optimum level from national celebrations since it is the occasion when everybody feels that my-ness towards one's nation.

Q.6 Why do you think some people think that national celebrations are a waste of government's money? Would you agree or disagree with this view? Why?

Some people express their dislike towards the expenditure incurred during the national celebrations. They hold the view that this extravaganza is for no practical purpose and the money spent will go in vain. Instead, the same amount should be used for some constructive motives like spreading environmental awareness, poverty removal etc. However convincing and irrefutable these arguments may sound, I firmly disagree with their belief. Everything cannot be counted in terms of money. Every patriotic citizen has the right to indulge in the wild celebrations in the national events that too of the significance of an independence day. Certain feelings have the importance which can and should never be evaluated in economic terms.

Interview 29

Part One:

1)How often do you watch television ? (why/why not)

Nowadays, television has become the most common source of entertainment. Honestly speaking, I do not spend more time watching television as I have some more exciting and educative sources of passing time. I watch some selected programmers. I somehow manage to steal time in the evening, especially for news. I personally do not find television to be an effective source of entertainment. Since so many channels offer so many programmes throughout the day, we sometimes get confused as to what to see and what to avoid. Eventually we end up not watching a single programme perfectly.

2) Which television channel do you usually watch? (Why?)

Whenever I have leisure time, I watch news on television. My favourite news channel is TIMES NOW. To my mind, it is the most authentic and reliable news source. I find all the news reported on that channel to be absolutely unbiased and not spiced up. Besides that, all the news reporters and journalists seem to be well trained in the English language as all of them speak flawless English. The way it dissects and analyses the myths regarding the current events is really worth imitating for other news channels. Watching TIMES NOW has helped me not only in remaining in touch with current events but to improve my English language skills as well.

3) Do you enjoy the advertisements on television? (Why / why not?)

I do enjoy but not all the advertisements. In the time of stiff competition, many companies have come up with very innovative and hard-to-believe kind of advertisements. I really love watching such advertisements. Another factor is that we get a chance to have glimpses of many sports and movie stars through advertisements. Since stars are hired to endorse almost all the famous brands. I really do not appreciate silly and themeless advertisements. I like the advertisements of automobile companies especially when they introduce a new car in the market. All resources of knowledge of how to make the best advertisements are exploited in order to make the car a big hit among people.

4) Do you think most programmes on television are good? (why/why not?)

I think nobody would completely agree with this idea. It is not for no reason that television is often termed as an idiot box. I vehemently express my dislike for almost a l the reality shows except some truly decent programmes like KBC, some talent shows etc. Public display of obscenity in those reality shows affects the people from cultural point of view. Even daily soaps are boring and telecast unrealistic stories. I am a die hard fan of relaxing comedy soaps and some informative programmes. Apart from all these, I admire all the news channels. In brief, I would say there are very rare programmes which deserve the adjective 'good'.

Part Two:

Describe a friend of your family you remember from your childhood.
Say:
Who the person was...
How your family knew this person...
How often this person visited your family and explain why you remember this person...

Ans:

Some people have extremely inspiring personalities. Their very existence or presence ooze love, trust and confidence. I am saying this because the person I am going to describe was such one. I not only remember but miss very badly the friend of my mother. She was Nirali aunty, the best friend of my mother and a selfless supporter of my family in all the circumstances.

Unfortunately she passed away two years back but we feel her undying affection and love for us. The reason why she became close to our family is that she was a childhood friend of my mother and co incidentally both of them got married in the same city. Perhaps both were destined to accompany each other throughout the life. It was only through my mother that we all came to know about her. She was little younger than my mother so we came in her contact after her marriage. I don't remember any day when she hadn't paid any visit to my house. So far as I recollect, she was at the helm of affairs whenever there was any function in my family-- social or whatsoever. The fact that we were living in the same society and she didn't have any social relative in the city brought her even closer to my mom and to all of us. As a person, she was wonderful and down to earth. Her gregarious nature made her personality more pleasing. I remember her for two important reasons. One was that she used to assist me a lot in my school homework and completing assignments. The other was her playful nature. Frankly speaking, she had never let me feel that she was older than me in the age.

Total dedication to work and unconditional commitment to family are the two great values I imbibed from her. She was quite outspoken and perhaps that was the reason she sometimes appeared apparently harsh but she was very delicate from within. She had played a great role in my upbringing. Since my mother was a teacher professionally, I used to spend maximum time of the day with her. She had made very deep and subtle impacts on my delicate mind as a kid. I consider myself so fortunate that I got the highest time to spend with her. Today also, whenever she happens to strike my mind, my eyes turn to tears.

Part Three:

Q.1 What do you think makes someone a good friend to a whole family?

To become a friend to an individual is not such a tough task but to become good friend to an entire family is undoubtedly not an easy job. First of all the person must have a mingling nature with all the members of the family and should be acceptable to all. The main thing is that he should know well when to remain within limits and when to have his say in the family matters. He should refrain from offering unsolicited advices. A family friend is one who always ensures that all the members remain united and one. It is the duty of a family friend to resolve any friction if it appears in the family he or she is related to. This requires good communication skills. Being **a** good communicator alone won't help until one has won the trust of all.

Q.2 Do you think we meet different kinds of friends at different stages of our lives? In what ways are these types of friend different ?

It is an obvious fact that we meet the friends of various kinds at different stages of our life.

Friends we meet at various stages of life are diverse from many aspects. As we grow and develop in our life, our roles also keep changing accordingly. These new roles bring us in contact with different people and we form friendships with them. The main factor is age. In our childhood, we have the friends of the same age. Elders certainly enjoy the company of elders. Youngsters like youngsters only. The kind of behaviour and interaction also change over time. We do not behave with the friends in our profession in the same manner we used to do with our childhood friends. School time friends, college time friends, business friends, club friends are some of the examples of how we build friendship with variety of people.

Q.3 How easy is it to make friends with people from a different age? group?

In my opinion, it takes considerable amount of time to establish friendly relation with the person who is either older or younger than us. The main reason is the mindset. Specific age group is influenced by his or her own time. The time during which they grew up, the kind of environment they have got during schools, their fashions are bound to be different. Friendship is formed only when two people share something common with each other. And it is difficult to get that commonness between two people who were born and brought up in two different times. Though I believe that it is not impossible for the flower of friendship to blossom between two people of different ages, it also depends on the person who extends the proposal of friendship. Mingling and loquacious kind of people make friends easily. Age factor is certainty a hindrance but not insurmountable one. It is not uncommon to see in the society that two people make **a** good pair of friends despite having quite a big difference of age. If two individuals share a common passion or hobby, they can become good friends irrespective of time they were born in.

Q.4 Do you think it is possible to be friends with someone if you never meet them in person? Is this real friendship?

It is possible in the world of technology. The main mediums of building relations and keeping in touch are social networking sites. If you consistently converse with somebody for a long period of time and find the person to be a reliable one, friendship can be built regardless of whether you have met each other in person anytime or not. Undoubtedly technology has denied boundaries. But the question is, will there be an element of commitment? How can a person be relied upon just by verbal commitment? Real friendship is totally a sacred and selfless relation. Making relation just to get rid of your loneliness can not be and should not be mistaken for friendship. Real friends are rare to find.

Q.5 What kind of influence can friends have on our lives?

It is not for nothing that a proverb came into existence that "Man is known by the company he keeps". Friends exert tremendous influence on us. Knowingly or unknowingly, we get affected. The effect can be of any nature. Good friends always strive to make us free from evils if we have any. Bad friends always corrupt us morally. Friends even influence our belief system i.e. ideology. Influential friends tend to dominate our belief system. If friends happen to be from different cultural or religious background, it also plays a role though subtly. The attitudes and problem solving abilities of some friends also influence the rest of the friends.

Q.6 How important would you say it is to have friends from different cultures?

It is not in our hands to decide at what stage who will enter in our lives and will occupy an important place as friends. Friendship knows no barriers of culture or religion. I don't think that having the friends from diverse cultural backgrounds will help a lot. Friends are friends. I think friends are universally same. Perhaps it is the only relation which can be defined in the universally acceptable terms. The only advantage of having the friend of different cultures is that we will get to know the social life of a new culture and we will know altogether different perspective of evaluating different episodes of life. New language, dressing sense, rituals, food and norms of social behaviour are some of the things we can know.

Interview 30

Part One:

1) What kinds of things make people laugh? (why/why not?)

Laughter is caused when something unusual and unexpected things take place without any serious consequences. For example if somebody falls down in a funny manner while sitting in the chair, it causes laughter. But one will never laugh if the persons get injured after falling down. Some people have exceptionally fun loving nature. Being in the company of such kind of people makes us laugh uninhibitedly. Nowadays we can see the trend of joining laughing clubs. People are seen laughing while watching comedy soaps or movies.

2) Do you like making others laugh?

Not usually. But when we all friends meet casually for just parties or movies, we laugh a lot and I am always a leader in initiating the laughing campaign. Specifically I like to make my friends laugh when they are in stressful situations. My family members always prefer to have their dinner with me because it is me who makes their dinner excellent by passing some funny comments which make them laugh a lot. I can't make unacquainted people or strangers laugh.

3) Do you think it is important for people to laugh? (why/why not?)

Absolutely yes. Laughing has both physical and psychological advantages. When a person laughs whole heartedly, his throat and respiratory system get good exercise and as a result blood circulation in the affected organs becomes faster. Besides physical benefits, it helps bust the stress which is a very pernicious problem of modern society. A person always feels better when he or she laughs. Nowadays, laughing is emerging as an independent therapy and it is now a proven fact that laughing helps the patient recover fast from his or her existing ailments.

I think it is very important to laugh if a person wants to lead a fulfilling life. But I vehemently despise it if somebody laughs unnecessarily and without any reason. Such behaviour is a symptom of not being psychologically fit and healthy.

4) Is laughing the same as feeling happy?

Laughter is not a happy feeling but it is an expression when a person feels happy. If any normal human being is seen laughing, one can predict that he or she must be happy. Expressions are universally common. Though some people can remain stable in all kinds of feelings but I think it is healthy to express all kinds of feelings. So laughing is not feeling happy but it is like feeling happy because without feeling happy a person normally does not laugh. Nowadays people laugh a lot in the morning in laughing clubs and try to remove their stress but that is altogether a different phenomenon.

Part Two:

Describe an idea you had for improving something at work or college.
Say...
When and where you had your idea...
What your idea was...
Who told you about your idea and explain why you thought your idea would make an improvement...

Ans.

I am fond of listening to spiritual discourses because they offer very motivating ideas to make our life more meaningful and fulfilling. I would here like to speak on the idea which has completely changed my life and can prove to be a recipe of success for others too. I don't recollect the exact time but it was approximately five to six years back that I heard Yoga Guru Swami Ramdev live on the stage in Ahmedabad. In his discourse while performing Yoga, he gave a stirring thought to be successful in all the aspects of life. He said, "Live in the present and whatever you do, do it with complete focus and faith without expecting results "it requires just a minute to verbalize the thought but it takes many months to put it into practice.

I started implementing it and was really awestruck to find that it was showing its results from the first day. I started doing my studies with total commitment. The main benefit I got was that I no longer get distracted from my work. Previously I was bit fickle minded and very easily got distracted even at the slightest temptation. Now I don't even pick telephone without finishing my task. I have realized that most of our energy is spent in expecting fruits of the work. If a person doesn't care about the result of his work, his all the senses and total energy will get focused on the given work. And if it happens, result is bound to be good. Another thing was that we hardly live in present. We either get lost in the past or keep planning the future. If we take care of our present, future will automatically take care of itself. After putting this idea into the practice, I noticed that I started getting very good marks in my annual exams. I realized that I would never get good marks by worrying about my result. The only way out is to focus on present and work hard. The ideas given by Swami Ramdev do not apply to me only. I believe they are universally tried, tested and trusted principles of success. If anybody sincerely makes efforts to follow these ideas, I believe a person can live happily. Keep aside professional success, they will help us live a happy and pleasant life. For example, when we eat our food while watching television, we can neither enjoy the taste nor watch the programme perfectly. It is better to do one thing at given time. By doing many things simultaneously, we waste our energy and do not get desired result either.

Part Three:

Q.1 Some people think that education should be about memorizing the important ideas of the past. Do you agree or disagree? Why?

The term education is very broad and encompassing. Merely storing the information of the past and unnecessarily burdening the mind can never be an ideal education. Certainly students should be taught about the past and history but at the same time they should also be taught how to interpret the information in order to learn new lessons from it. Learning about past is as important as learning from past. Person can avoid repeating the same blunders if they are aware of the history. Apart from this, education means a lot more. Imparting the knowledge of technology and other important subjects of life should also be taught. If we go by the beliefs of some prominent thinkers of the world, the main role of education should be to ensure the moral well being of the students.

Q.2 Should education encourage students to have their own new ideas? Why?

Absolutely. I personally believe that education is not merely passing on the information from one person to another one. Students must be prepared to think own their own. It is only when students are encouraged to freely express their own opinion and critically evaluate them that we can hope to produce great brains. The problem with modern education system is that it teaches to accept whatever is taught to them. Students are never taught to question and doubt. Perhaps that is the reason why we have failed to produce another Gandhi, Einstein or Vivekananda. I firmly believe that new ideas should be welcomed with open arms and students must be encouraged to develop critical thinking.

Q.3 How do you think teachers could help students to develop and share their own ideas?

The role of a teacher is not limited to only preparing students to perform well in examinations but it goes beyond that. First a teacher must get rid of their archetype image of being so strict and unapproachable. Teachers must behave in a friendly manner with students and appreciate their ideas however silly or idiotic they appear apparently. A real teacher is one who comes down to the level of the student, sees through his eyes and understands through his mind. This attitude of teachers makes students comfortable with them. Many students with innovative ideas fail to develop themselves just because their thinking abilities are suppressed and nipped in the bud. Their ideas should be evaluated keeping in mind their age, level of maturity and level of education they have gone through. Another way of encouraging the thinking ability of students is by changing the process of teaching. A teacher should adopt interactive ways of teaching.

Q.4 Should employers encourage their workers to have new ideas about improving the company? Why?

I believe that good companies always function in a democratic manner. Workers are practically involved in the actual working environment of the company so their suggestions and ideas are bound to be realistic. It is often seen that workers too have sometimes innovative and revolutionary ideas which if implemented will accelerate the growth of the company. Employees should be made to think freely and give their feedbacks. Such kind of environment in the company also helps the employer win the loyalty of his employees. All manpower-- right from the CEO to the office boy-- can contribute to the development of the company or organization, if their ideas are appreciated and they are given perquisites if their ideas are found to be applicable.

Q.5 Do you think people sometimes dislike ideas just because they are new? Why?

People hardly think in an unorthodox manner. There is a sense of security in following tried and tested formulas. New ideas are always looked down upon and they are doubted. People raise suspicions over their applicability and success. The history is the witness that society has taken a lot of time in accepting an out of the box philosophy. Even the pioneers of new ideas had to go through a lot of protest and opposition. Many scientists were burnt alive in Europe if their beliefs were found to be in conflict with those of the Bible's. People feel reserved in accepting new ideas because they are scared of their general acceptability.

Q.6 What is more difficult: having new ideas or putting them into practice? Which is more important for a successful company?

I think both are difficult. Most of the companies run in an orthodox manner but very few companies invest heavily just to find new ideas. Getting new ideas require many things—like a lot of study, investment, learning approach by employers, conducting surveys, eliciting feedbacks from employees etc. but merely getting new ideas will be of no help if they are not properly implemented. Implementation of new ideas is a very tough task particularly if it is in a company. It sometimes calls for administrative and technical changes as well. Training manpower to adapt to new changes is equally important for better implementation. One can not single out as to what is more important but one thing is for sure that putting new ideas into practice is more challenging. Both the things are important for any company to run successfully.

Interview 31

Part One:

1) Have you ever been in the cold weather? (When)

Once I visited a very famous hill station when it was the dead of winter. The place is located on the boundary of Rajasthan which geographically locks my state i.e. Gujarat. I didn't expect the winter to be so chilling there. I went there before a year. I am not used tc living in extreme weather conditions. I was literally shivering despite having worn good woolen clothes. Frankly admitting, it was a nice experience.

2) How often is the weather cold where you come from?

We experience three seasons throughout the year. Winter season during which we feel the coldest climate lasts about three to four months from November to the beginning of February. The average temperature during winter remains 15 to 20 degree Celsius.

3) Are some parts of your country colder than others? (Why)

India is geographically so diverse a nation that the weather conditions are bound to remain different. Some parts of the country are land locked with other regions while some are near sea. Some are in wood and some are in plains and rocks. Weather varies considering geographic location. Regions land locked with other regions naturally experience severer winter than those located on sea. Season cycle also gets affected.

4) Would you prefer to live in a hot place or a cold place? (Why)

My preference is cold place. It is an evident truth that people living in cold places are healthier than those living in hot places. In cold climate, the digestive system also works well. We feel vitality and energy throughout the day. I believe that climate affects one's nature and mood as well. In cold climate, we feel energetic and can work tirelessly for longer hours. We can do exercise for longer time. Our skin also remains dry which results into attractive complexion. We can enjoy the delicate rays of sun which are rich in vitamin D.

Part Two:

Describe a famous person that has / had great influence on the people of your country.

Say.

country...

Who that person is...

What that person did...

How you feel about that person and consider whether or not that person will continue to be an influence in the future...

Ans:

There are so many famous people in our country who are literally hero worshipped by people.

Here I would like to speak about a very well known social activist Anna Hzare. His actual name is Babulal Hazare but people lovingly call him Anna Hazare. He has caught the imagination of the entire middle class by launching many campaigns against corruption which has become an evil in all the public spheres. His main fight is for introducing the ombudsman i.e Lokpal bill to curb corruption in Government sectors. He several times observed an indefinite fast and got arrested for the security reasons. All the time he went on a fast, he received huge and unprecedented public support. All the civil society leaders and social activists accepted his leadership and expressed the solidarity. By the dint of his impeccable character, he has emerged as the most powerful leader of the civil society after Gandhiji, in whom people have immense faith. Since people find him the man of incredible integrity, he manages to receive tremendous public support whenever he launches a protest or agitation. Despite having served in Indian army, he is committed to the values of Truth and non violence. His agitations are non violent in nature. Without holding any constitutional or political position, he always has a bigger sway in the policies framed by government for public welfare. I personally feel that he must carry on the legacy of Mahatma Gandhi. He has galvanized an organized public voice and this is very important in any democratic country to keep the government constantly vigilant ant aware of its constitutional responsibilities. I believe he has successfully reminded government of its accountability to the people by exposing the corrupt practices of it. He also had a bigger say in drafting Right To Information act.

I believe Annaji will continue to receive the same response in the future as people see a great ray of hope in him. People have been suffering the pains of food inflation and frequent price hike of fuels. He is also considering to carry out other campaigns if government doesn't listen to his demands of enacting two more laws i.e. right to recall and right to reject.

Part Three:

Q.1 Famous people often become role models for teenagers. How significant is this?

Role model is one whom one aspires to be like. One should not become a role model just because he dominates the newspaper headlines or enjoys a good screen space on television. Being famous doesn't vouch for person's being good. Notoriety should not be mistaken for reputation because nowadays people earn the name more by controversies and less due to character and integrity. I don't see anything wrong in making a famous person the role model. But one should not be swayed just by an amount of fame the concerned person enjoys. But if we look at the thought process of modern generation, they believe that a person should have an excellence in the matter for which he has become a role model. The rest of the things matter less.

Q.2 Do actors and models get too much attention in the media?

People especially youngsters hold keen interest in knowing even the silliest matters in regard to actors and models. Media simply panders to these aspirations of people and by doing so they will get the highest TRP. Glamour world exerts tremendous awe effect on youngsters. If we talk from other perspective there is cut-throat competition. Many electronic channels are exclusively broadcasting news only. When they have nothing to offer, they come up with special shows revealing the lifestyles of actors and models. Newspapers also publish such news just to cover up the space. The attention they are getting is not only more but undeserving too in my opinion.

Q.3 Should people lose the right to privacy just because they are famous?

It is usually expected and to certain extent it is desirable too. A person enjoying a great name should be above and beyond doubt. If a person enjoys huge popularity, he should be willing to make that sacrifice. There is nothing like a free lunch in this world. The basic reason is that people should not be betrayed in the name of freedom and privacy. However I believe that unnecessary and constant watch of media over one's private life is the violation of basic human right. Every person should have the complete right over his private life. Success in professional life must not rob an individual of his privacy. He should be allowed to lead his life in his own terms. Simultaneously famous people should not abuse this freedom.

Q.4 If you could meet anyone famous (dead or alive) who would it be and why?

Without a second thought, I would prefer meeting Mr. Atal Bihari Vajpeyee. The main reason is that he is my all time favourite public figure. He had held many high offices including the highest constitutional post that is the office of prime minister but he had led completely spotless public life. He was a rare blending of a successful poet and a visionary politician. He was an exceptionally gifted orator and I have developed my public speaking skills keeping him as my ideal. His dedication was unsurpassable. He remained single throughout his life just to serve the nation. I would consider myself fortunate if I get an opportunity to meet him at least once in my lifetime.

Q.5 In your opinion, do certain personality types handle fame or attention better than others?

Famous people have to live in public life and constantly interact with various kinds of people. They are under public eye. All the famous people can not handle this enormous public attention and get exposed even at the slightest mistake. People who are good readers of mass psychology can handle fame better as they know well what to do and more importantly what to avoid in public life. A famous person must be a good communicator because it is the speech which is strength and weakness both depending upon what words a person chooses to speak. That is the reason politicians, movie stars and social leaders tend to manage their public life successfully.

Q.6 Do you feel there should be restriction placed on actors according to their age and sex?

Artists should enjoy unbridled freedom to explore their full potential. But the freedom should not be abused. I don't feel the need to impose any restriction to regulate their public behaviour considering their age. But one thing is for sure that it is often found that some unsuccessful female actors indulge in unacceptable physical exposure in their desperate desire for success. Such kind of brazen public display of obscenity must not be allowed under any circumstances. Even established actresses are seen resorting to such petty gimmicks for cheap publicity. If such blatant aberrations are nipped in the bud, the society can salvage its traditional values.

Interview 32

Part One:

1) How do you usually travel to work or college? (Why)

The mode of transport I prefer is my two wheeler i.e. bike to commute to my college. Though there is good facility of public transportation, I use my bike not for no reason. Since the punctuality of public transport is as reliable as the weather forecast in monsoon, I use bike to reach college on time. Besides that, it gives me a sense of freedom. As the trend goes, it feels good to have your own swanky bike in college life and frankly speaking, that bike has become my identity.

2) Have you always traveled to wok / college in the same way? (Why / Why not)

I usually travel by my bike only but in exceptional cases, I go by bus. If vehicle is urgently needed at home and reason is also such that I can't deny, I have to leave my bike at home though I am so possessive about my bike. Sometimes I go on my friend's bike if there is a different plan of going to far way distances for party or a casual outing. It helps both of us to save the fuel cost. Such occasions are rare if I count.

3) What changes would improve the way you travel to work / college? (Why?)

Though I am completely satisfied with the way I travel, I would like to introduce certain changes. Even though the changes are not under my control, I believe they would make me travel in more thrilling manner. I am not happy with the road which I travel on. Cracks and ditches are too often. They do not let us travel freely and make us apply the brakes too often. It makes the travel expensive as vehicle consumes more fuel on such roads and sometimes we become the victim of severe backache. Another thing is that the road should be one way road so that we will witness less traffic congestion and it will make night traveling easier.

4) Do your mates travel in the same way?

Not necessarily. Depending on the financial affordability and availability of the kind of transport, the mode of transport varies. Some prefer public transport. Most of my friends have their own bikes as it is a fashion and trend as well. Many friends use their vehicles alternatively and travel together on the same bike in order to save the cost of the fuel.

Part Two:

Describe the main forms of transport in your hometown.
Say...
What the different forms of transport are...
How often you use them...
Which types of transport are most popular and consider whether or not the transportation systems are satisfactory...

Ans:

In my city being in the centre of Gujarat, we do not have water transport. Though I live in a capital city, we do not have any airport in the city since Ahmedabad is just 20 kilometers far from Gandhinagar and we can avail that facility very easily. Gandhinagar being the capital city and located in the centre of the state, we have wonderful road transport. Even public transport is very competitive and managed in a very professional manner. We have so many buses every day connecting my city with rest of the country. We have an excellent inter city transportation system with good frequency of buses, which connects all the parts of the city. One can find good number of private taxies too but it is bit expensive hence less preferred by middle class. I having my own vehicle, rarely travel by public transport but sometimes out of compulsion, I have to travel by it. Most popular form of transport is private transport. My city is home to government employees and people normally possess their own vehicles. But there is a considerable number of people relying upon public transport, especially those who work out of the city, since the frequency of buses and trains is really good. They come on time. Gandhinagar being one of the least congested with traffic on road, daily commuters traveling by public transport can comfortably attend their work on time. Trains connecting almost all the major cities of India pass through my city so people can have the alternative when they are supposed to travel to far-flung areas.

The only despicable thing about public transport is the condition of buses. Cleanliness is ignored and buses are not maintained on time to time basis. As a consequence, buses can break down in the middle and this is the reason why public transport especially road transport has failed to emerge as the most preferred form of transport. If buses are maintained well and kept clean, they will certainly attract more people.

Part Three:

Q.1 What are benefits of traveling by public transport?

Above everything, public transport is the safest form of transport. Moreover, in comparison with private forms of transport, the fare is significantly cheaper. In case of vehicular beak down, all the travelers are easily accommodated in other vehicle and if it doesn't happen, entire amount of fare is given back to the travelers. In case of accident, minor or fatal, all the travelers are given compensation to meet the medical expenditure. Family members of the deceased ones also get the compensation by government for the maintenance of the family.

Q.2 Air traveling is gradually becoming very popular among people. Why is it so?

Air traveling is the safest and least time consuming mode of travel. Nowadays, it has becomea need in the time of global economy where people value time above money. Aviation sector has developed in the recent time. As a consequence, infrastructure and frequency have remarkably improved. Investment-friendly policies of Government have lured many private players to play a key role and hence the sector has become more competitive making the benefits more alluring. All the factors have been well accompanied by increasing buying power of the people.

Q.3 In what ways can governments encourage people to use public transport?

Launching new schemes will not work if existing ills are not addressed first. Three things stop people from using public transport. Poor frequency, absence of cleanliness and lack of punctuality. Addressing these three areas must be the first priority. Government has to make public transport more competitive in order to survive from tough competition by private sector. Good facilities can be made available. And the number of travelers should not exceed the number of seats available. For elite passengers, air conditioned buses can be introduced. Vehicles must be maintained on timely basis. Increasing connectivity with all the major areas of the country will attract more passengers.

Q.4 Having too many cars on our roads causes air pollution. What are some of the other causes of air pollution?

Vehicles contribute more to air pollution. Besides, we cannot deny blind industrialization. Chemical industries emit poisonous gases in the air which pollutes the air. Increasing use of crackers is also the reason for air pollution. Nowadays crackers are used in almost all the social and religious occasions. Nowadays, it is proven by the science that the use of electronic gadgets like air conditioners, mobiles too causes air pollution. Improper disposal of waste too pollutes the air sometimes.

Q.5 How are eco-friendly practices encouraged in your country?

CNG has been made more preferable fuel which is totally eco friendly. Public transport is being innovatively revamped in order to decrease the number of vehicles on the road. People are discouraged to use plastic which is very dangerous for environment and encouraged to use recyclable material. Mass awareness is generated in order to persuade people to use water economically and to turn off lights and electrical equipment when they are not in use. Financial assistance is provided to those who prefer to install solar plants in their homes as solar energy is called one of the promising natural sources of energy.

Q.6 Sciences can be used to develop environmentally – friendly alternatives. In what ways can this be done?

Science can be used to harness the most promising and infinite sources of energy like wind and solar energy. Solar panels should absorb the maximum solar energy. Science should bring about a new automobile revolution by replacing petroleum with hydrogen and solar energy as the fuel. Environmental damage caused by maritime transport can also be averted by doing more scientific research in the concerned areas. Maximum research should take place with a view to exploiting unconventional sources of energy.

Interview 33

Part One:

1)What would you suggest a visitor should see and do in your country?

India is well known for its historical and religious places. However I would advise any stranger to visit the places of spiritual significance. These places enhance our composure and give mental peace to all the visitors and are rich treasure of spiritual knowledge. I will also insist on paying visits to historical places too as they speak volumes of the pinnacle our ancestors had reached in terms of artistic development like science of architecture, sculpture etc. in addition to that, I would urge the visitor to participate in all the festivals and social celebration n order to have the glimpse into the traditional culture of India.

2) Are there any traditional arts or music you would recommend?

India has made unimaginable explorations in terms of art and music. I would strongly recommend the visitors to listen to the classical music and songs especially of Sufi sort. Music and arts have always remained an inseparable part of Indian spirituality.

3) Tell me about the kind of foreign visitors or tourists who go to your country.

India being very cultural and traditional country has abundance of places which reveal the renowned Indian culture. Visitors wishing to have a glimpse of that come to India. People across the world come here and even make India their abode to seek spiritual pleasures since India are the home to almost all the spiritual disciplines like Yoga, Nyay, Vaisheshik etc. Places rich in natural beauty and of historical importance also fascinate considerable number of foreign tourists.

4) In what ways has tourism changed your country?

Frankly talking, tourism has been opening newer avenues of development. New sources of employment generation have come up. Tourism is one of the main sources of generating revenue for the states like Rajasthan, Uttarakhand and Chhattisgadh etc. Constantly increasing flow of tourists have made the authorities improve the concerned areas like transportation, banking, hospitality etc. Besides that, domestic products and items have found global market. Tourism has had wide ranging impacts on my country.

Part Two:

A natural disaster or calamity you have seen or heard about.
Say...
When and where it happened...
What the disaster was...
What was the damage caused...
How you felt...

Ans:

Entire Gujarat was caught unaware on 26th January 2001 when it was hit by a deadly earth quake. Coincidently it was the republic day and the quake shook the Gujarat when all the people were engrossed in the celebration of republic day at 8.30 a.m. The epicentre was Bhachau Taluka of Kutch region which witnessed the highest destruction but tumours were felt across the state. The earth reached the magnitude of between 7.6 to 7.7 rector scales. It was the historic in the sense that Gujarat had never seen the disaster of such immense gravity and magnitude before. If we go by the reported data, nearly 20,000 people lost their lives and above 1, 50,000 people received serious injuries. The figure might have been much more considering the fact that many corpses were not in the position to establish the identity and many deaths were unreported.

Entire Kutch region was totally devastated. There were only defeaning screams of affected people. People were left homeless. It took almost six years for Kutch to revive and restore normal life. But the way international community came to co operate in rescue and relief operations is absolutely appreciable. I felt very horrible since it was first time that I saw so many dead people at a time. The scenes of people screaming for food and help was very pathetic." How helpless man is in front of nature!!! "Everybody was feeling the same. I was worried about my relatives and friends in that region. Fortunately nobody was affected but almost all the relatives lost their shelter. One of my friends lost his grandfather in that fatal tragedy.

Part Three:

Q.1 What are the various measures that are usually taken to help the affected?

The first and foremost measure that is undertaken is rescue operations. Aerial surveys are conducted in order to assess the gravity of the situation. The things of daily needs like food packets, clothing are sent to the affected site. In addition to that emergency medical facility is made available to treat the injured people. If the devastation is too big then arrangement for mass cremation is also made.

Q.2 How can a country be prepared to deal with such calamities?

There must be powerful and well equipped disaster management system. Concerned nation can adopt the ready made technology which is in use to the areas prone to certain disasters. For example, earthquake is not new to Japan so they have invented technologies to fight with the disaster. Any country can avail that without wasting more money in research and development. Well trained team of personnel ever ready to conduct immediate rescue measures should be there. Departments like meteorology, seismology should be made more competent in their prediction of disasters. People living in the areas prone to such calamities must be made capable enough to be prepared to take certain immediate measures.

Q.3 Have you ever experienced any natural calamity in your hometown? How did people react to it?

The people in my area are not used to facing such calamities. The only disaster we witnessed is destructive floods before four years. People got scared and could not think in the poised manner during that disaster. I think people of my locality are poorly equipped to face such natural challenges. Every time monsoons set in, people start remembering those tragic stories of flood. Since that tragedy, monsoon brings panic. But one thing is certain that people of my town are always ready to extend their support and assistance to those affected anywhere.

Q.4 What do you think the role of media is during such events ?

Media plays a substantial role during such tragic events. Wide ranging and constant coverage of the events incite sympathy for the affected all over the world. But I strongly express my reluctance when victims are sometimes embarrassed when their individual stories are highlighted on national channels. Media many times does a commendable job by exposing inabilities of government to tackle such exigencies. They draw the attention of people to the most demanding aspects of the tragedies. They sometimes help victims to reach out to their dear and near ones in case they are lost or missing.

Q.5 With news about calamities every day, do you think we tend to forget them too quickly?
It is often that people forget the tragedies too quickly. Public memory is too short in such matters. The reason is more than evident. In recent years, the number of disasters either natural or man made have considerably increased. Frequently occurring rail and road accidents, terrorist attacks, natural disasters have become day to day phenomenon and constant flow of sensational news gradually make people less sensitive towards them. Events which cause a big human loss and material damage certainly make people feel bad and sympathetic towards fellow citizen or even those across the border but this sympathy last as long as the bubble lasts. But still I believe people do their level best in reaching out to the affected in emergencies.

Q.6 What is the role of international aids in times of distress?
Natural disasters are not specific to particular regions though some parts of the world are prone to some disasters. For example earth quake in Japan is very common. International aids can help the affected region revive faster and restore the normalcy sooner. All the countries can not have enough machinery or expertises to combat all the disasters. The countries well equipped in tackling particular disaster can make their experience and technology readily available to the affected area. Financial assistance offered by international community also plays vital role considering the fact that all the countries are not sound enough from economic point of view to fight with an uninvited tragedy.

Interview 34

Part One:

1) What would you like to change in your daily routine?
I think there isn't any room for making any change since my daily schedule is perfectly worked out to justify my daily commitments like going to college, attending coaching classes, helping my father in his work in the evening. Frankly speaking, I don't wish to alter my working schedule as it gives me an ample time for unwinding. Despite this, I believe that I can't spare enough time for my daily exercise. Given the chance and opportunity, I would like to start my day bit later so that I can spend more time to do Yoga and other exercise.

2) Are all your days same?
Weekdays are more or less almost same barring occasional alterations due to emergency, since college time is same everyday. Weekends come with a welcome relief since entire week abounds with monotony and boredom. Daily schedule gets disrupted only when we have different activities in the college to do like tournaments, exams, campus interviews etc. During vacations in Diwali and summer, we get a good chance to spend the time randomly.

3) Tell me about your typical weekdays and your typical weekend.

Weekdays are very typical considering the fact that we have to always do the same and monotonous work throughout the day. Going to college, attending lectures as per the schedule, gossiping with friends during a break, the only thing I like, coming back to home and again going to attend the coaching classes. I never know when the day gets over. My weekend is never typical. I plan my weekend in different ways. Honestly speaking, I like to spend my weekend randomly roaming here and there with friends.

4) What is the balance of study / work, and free time in your normal day?

My daily schedule is an ideal blending of study and free time which anybody would love to emulate. I daily spend two hours in the evening on sports which I have a great passion for. I believe this is an ideal time for unwinding and relaxing since it doesn't affect my studies but rejuvenates me to focus better on studies. However when there is conflict between study and games, I always give study a first preference. However I watch T.V. everyday, though only for half an hour.

Part Two:

A charitable work that you did / have been doing regularly.
Say...
When and where did you do that...
Who benefitted from it...
Why did you do it...
How you felt afterwards...

Ans:

Every person in the life gives charity. I am not so much a spiritual kind of person and don't give charity too often. The incident I am going to describe was one of its kinds. It was the first time that I offered selfless assistance to somebody. Once I was traveling in my car and my car broke down in the way and I had to bring my journey to the halt there. I called a mechanic and decided to have a rest there. There was a big and beautiful place exactly in front of the place where my car broke down. When I entered the place, I came to know that it was an orphanage where so many little children were playing. Listening to the tragic saga of all the children from the management, my heart really melted. I realized how unfortunate those innocent kids were who had not received the love and warmth of their parents. Some kids were abandoned just because they happened to be girls at the time of birth. I really took pity on them. I asked myself, "Why should these children go through this agony just because of their parent's fault? I decided to give 10,000 rupees as a charity and requested the authorities to get the children new school uniforms. I appreciated the management for really looking after the neglected section of society and providing them with the opportunities to grow like other kids of the mainstream society. I was really moved and I donated the money though I did not go there with that intention.

I took it as an opportunity to give back to society so I donated the amount without even asking my wife who was with me. I don't find appropriate words to express an irrepressible inner joy I felt on that day. I realized the worth of a selfless act. I understood the philosophy of giving back to society on that day. The spiritual ecstasy I felt on that day was really inexplicable. I realized that we have no right to indulge in exorbitant spending when so many fellow countrymen do not get sufficient means to keep their body and soul together.

Part Three:

Q.1 Do you think charity is important?
It is all about individual ideology. Charity is the best way to reach out the needy people in the true sense of the word. It is only by charity that needy section of society can survive and grow. It gives an immense pleasure to the giver and a sense of gratitude to the receiver. It is believed that by doing charitable deed; one can purify one's soul. All the religions of the world promote charity in one way or other.

Q. 2 What are the different sections of society which require charity?
There are various sections of society that are thrown out of mainstream and lead a very gloomy and dejected life. The reasons of being despondent and discarded vary from sections to sections. Disabled, mentally retarded, orphans, deserted elders, widows, abandoned women, physically and mentally abused people, drug addicts, victims of tragedy-- either natural or manmade are some of the kinds that are subject to constant torture and humiliation. As a consequence, they can't lead normal life. In order to bring them in the mainstream and make them realize that they are also as good as others, the charity is very important. Since such kind of people are usually considered to be the burden on the families and hence they are either abandoned or sent to any trust or organization that takes care of such people. To run such organizations for people leading a pathetic life, charity is of utmost importance to secure financial resources.

Q.3 Do people in your country do charity work on their own or contribute to charity organizations?
Some people do not trust the financial sanctity of some of the social organidsations. To some extent they are right because the news of financial irregularities within social organizations is not uncommon. Even spiritual organizations have not been spared from this evil. Why will people donate the money to any organization if there is no assurance of that money being used for the purpose which it has been given for? They don't want their hard earned money to go waste. It is all about the question of faith. But still people in my country always prefer to give charity through social or religious organizations of their respective faith since individual efforts have some limitation and can not bring concrete result.

Q.4 How can business houses contribute towards society?
Every business empire or a corporate house owes a lot to society. Without a balanced and supportive society, no business can develop. They can discharge their responsibility towards society by making schools for underprivileged children, providing jobs to those deserving yet unemployed, establishing industries in the rural areas, taking exclusive measures to protect environment, financially assisting the existing charity organizations etc. However the contribution of business sector should not be forgotten in generating employment for youth. If all the business and corporate houses adhere to the norms of environment and do not damage environment in their expansion spree, it would be the biggest service to society which is the need of an hour.

Q.5 Do you think charity and religion are related?

Not necessarily, but to major extent it is found that people having religious bent of mind are more involved in charity work and it is expected and understandable too. People having extreme faith in the existence of almighty and moral code of conduct hold the view that it is our duty to reach out to the needy people and even creatures because the world is the creation of God and He dwells everywhere so service to humanity is service to God. However all the people doing charity are not of the same belief, some people have sensitivity towards society and have sympathy for the disadvantaged sections of society. One can not live peacefully despite having abundant affluence if society is filled with evils. This ideology drives them to offer charity on regular basis.

Q.6 How important are social organizations for a society?

Individual efforts will not yield concrete results. The main role of social organizations is to organize the efforts made by people for the betterment of society. Efforts if not made in a collective manner will certainly fail to bring about expected results. Another very important role played by them is that they sometimes assist governments to frame policies in regard to the issues they work for. Even they exert justifiable pressure on government to rectify the errors in policy making or to make new policies. We are well aware of the efforts made by social organizations in spreading awareness regarding social issues and working out for the welfare of poor and downtrodden sections of society. In addition to that, social organizations provide nice platform to those who wish to dedicate their life and offer selfless services to society.

Interview 35

Part One:

1) Are your friends mostly your age or different ages? (Why?)

My all the friends are of my age as I hardly get time to mingle with others. But I think I can become a good friend to all since age is a factor but not a definitive one to build friendship. I have one good friend who is three to four years younger than me. We became friend on a cricket ground. It means two people having common interests can also become good friends.

2) Do you usually see your friends during the week or at weekend? (Why?)

I meet some of my friends in college. However there is not any fixed time when we meet. We occasionally plan outing together. We play cricket on sunday where I meet some friends on ground. But some friends studying out of the city rarely meet me as they come to the city only during vacations.

3) The last time you saw your friends, what did you do together?

It was the wedding of one of my friends. We all had a wild celebration there as it was after a long time that we all met one another. We all had a great time there bantering with one another. We all were given certain responsibility in the marriage. We danced a lot and fired crackers in the procession. Above all we all got nostalgic and had a good reminiscence about the days in the school.

4) In what ways are your friends important in our life?

I can't even imagine the life without friends. Life without friends will not be less than a hell, if I am not exaggerating. Friends are the rock solid support in the life especially in the times of tense situations. With great ease, they remove the tension. We miss them in good as well as adverse times. If friends are not there in celebrations, it would make us long for them. They make us feel lighter just by extending verbal support despite our being aware that solution to the problem is a remotest possibility for them.

Part Two:
Describe your favourite religious book.
Say...
Which the book is...
Why do you like...
What it is about...
Do you find it useful...

Ans:

All the religious books preach the message of love, peace and non violence but my choice is Geeta which is coincidentally my religious book too. I like Geeta not because it is my religious scripture but because of its uniqueness. Geeta is the only book in the world which was sung by GOD himself as Lord Krishna is popularly believed to have been the eighth incarnation of God. Perhaps it is the only book which was composed on a battlefield and it was a live conversation between two friends on the important puzzles of life and other philosophical complications. If we go by the opinions of the scholars of Sanskrit literature, Geeta was sung in an extraordinarily excellent artistic literary language. Geeta has an intensive depth of philosophy as it is based on eternal principles of life. An interesting thing is that though Geeta strongly advocates the eternity of soul and perishability of body, Lord Krishna motivated Arjuna to fight against his near and dear ones who were supporting evil. Any person who reads and understands the underlying theme of Geeta can't help becoming a devotee of Lord Krishna. Geeta preaches us the importance of selfless love and selfless work. The real beauty of Geeta lies in the consolations it offers to the layman. You need not be a great scholar or an erudite person in order to realize God. Any act done in a selfless manner and with the welfare of the world in mind takes you closer to Almighty. Constant feeling of nearness to God is the biggest devotion. I would like to emphasize here that nowhere in entire Geeta there is a mention of the word "HINDU" though it is the religious book of Hindus. It is for every human being who wants to lead a spiritually fulfilling and happy life. Geeta is not the Bible of Hinduism but it is the Bible of humanity. The principles in Geeta are so applicable in our daily life that anybody cutting across the boundaries of castes, religions and space will find them very beneficial. Geeta not only helps you in your spiritual quest but also empowers you to face the daily struggles of life. The theory of Karma and Selfless love helps one achieve success in the professional life as well. This universally appealing influence of Geeta truly makes it a universal book. It is the book which has been translated in almost all the major languages of the world not for propaganda but out of love for it.

Part Three:

Q.1 What is the importance of religion in our life?

Religion is the way which leads one closer towards the Almighty or realization of one's soul. Besides this, the highest goal of religion is to help one understand what is good and what is not, since everybody cannot be expected to have that discretionary power to make right judgments. Religion and religious teachings are the result of collective wisdom of millions of enlightened people though some of them appear redundant today. It is because of the fear, real or fictitious, instilled by religion that makes people follow moral values. Religious beliefs are thought to be unquestionable and questioning them is considered tantamount to blasphemy. Though religion is sometimes accused of hampering free thinking, its role in keeping moral values in society intact can never be overlooked.

Q.2 Why do you think spiritual books are more in demand nowadays?

People have seen the extreme results of materialism and consumerism. Since people across the world are becoming more intelligent day by day, they have equally become critical in their choice of life style. Self seeking and hedonistic life styles have led us nowhere. We run behind peace but peace seems to elude us. Now as people have witnessed the dire consequences of materialism, people have turned to spiritualism. Spirituality is believed to be giving enduring peace to all the honest seekers and hence it has found readers across the world. The increasing interest and awe of spirituality has naturally resulted into more buying of spiritual books and literature.

Q.3 Do you think religions breed extremism?

It is not the religion which breeds extremism but it is the misleading interpretation of religious teaching which leads to fanaticism. No religion can ever condone the act of violence in any form and if it does so, it is not worthy to be called a religion. All religions teach us divine values like love, peace, non violence, compassion etc. Some politically motivated people distort the religious teaching to suit their vested interests. They poison the minds of people by proving other religions to be threat to their identity. This is the way extremism takes birth. Two religions can never be paradoxical in their aims of establishing a divine order in the world. Philosophies might differ and so called religious leaders take advantages of that.

Q.4 Youngsters take less interest in religions. Is it good?

It is the result of increasing education. Modern youth will never accept anything which doesn't hold appeal to their intellect. They always question the established beliefs and if religion fails to answer their questions, it will never interest them. It is only because some existing religious traditions cannot stand scientific scrutiny, they will not accept them. But all the beliefs cannot be discarded just because some of them fail to stand the scrutiny of science. Youngsters must understand the positive aspects of religions. Every tradition has an underlying philosophy. Without understanding why a specific tradition came into existence, discarding it is no less than arrogance and a grave stupidity.

Q.5 Are religions harmful to a nation?

If we look into the history of the world, we would realize that maximum blood has been shed in the name of religion. Religions in their essence can never harm anybody but the tragedy is that religions have become a political tool garnering more popular support in most of the democracies. Frequently occurring riots and terrorist attacks are the result of growing religious fundamentalism. During elections, religious identities are exploited to get maximum votes. Religious minorities make a huge vote bank in democratic countries. Religions have made more damage than contribution in national life. Religions have always escalated tensions in placing instead of easing them which is their actual role.

Q.6 Whom can one call a spiritual person?

People usually mistake being spiritual for being religious. Spirituality has nothing to do with external things like one's clothes; appearance etc. Spirituality is all about one's individual development as a human. The person who bears malice towards none and holds charity for all can be termed as a spiritual person. Such people are always law abiding and are of high moral values. They are always positive about life and see the hand of Almighty or nature in whatever happens around them.

Interview 36

Part One:

1) What kinds of food do you like to eat?

I usually like to eat my traditional food which consists mostly dal, rice, chapattis, green vegetable and pulses. Moreover, I really prefer eating sweets. I am not a gourmet who holds the taste for various foods. However I like eating Punjabi and Chinese foods occasionally. I am a strong advocate of vegetarian food though I eat eggs when winter is at its peak.

2) What kinds of new food would you like to try? (Why?)

I have heard a lot about Italian, Thai and Mexican food. I don't know exactly whether any non vegetarian ingredients are used in making them or not. I would really wish to taste them on the condition that they are purely vegetarian. I appreciate all the new items which my wife prepares learning from a recipe book.

3) Do you like cooking? (Why?)

Honestly speaking, I have very strong dislike for cooking. I had tried cooking once and later decided not to cook ever as I found it to be really a difficult job. One has to remember so many things while cooking. I believe cooking is a serious act since a small error can spoil the taste and sometimes affect the health of all the people who eat the same food. This thing really scares me a lot.

4) Do you prefer home-cooked food or food from restaurants? (Why?)

I like only home made food due to many reasons. First of all, we cannot deny the factor of cleanliness and hygiene. I believe the food is not just the mixture of ingredients prepared for eating; the affection with which it is cooked does affect the taste. Home made food is cooked considering our requirements and standard of health. However, I am not against gorging on the food in a restaurant occasionally. Frankly speaking, I always find excuses to go to a restaurant.

Part Two:

Describe an interest or hobby that you enjoy.
say:
How you became interested in it...
How long you have been doing it...
Why you enjoy it and explain what benefits you get from this interest or hobby...

Ans:
I have an inclination for many good activities like traveling, tasting various foods, playing volleyball, watching motivational movies. But my all time favourite pastime is reading because pursuit of knowledge is my passion. There is a very strange incident which made me a voracious reader. I skipped the test of mathematics in my ninth standard and was caught red handed by my father. In order to teach me a lesson so that I never repeat the same mistake in future, he made me read book named "Satya Na Prayogo" (My Experiments with Truth) at one go. It was the collection of some parts of the autobiography of our nation's father, Mahatma Gandhi. From that day onwards, I developed a great penchant for reading. I found that books are really interesting. I really wish to express my heartfelt gratitude to my father for having punished me. Love for reading has helped me in my academic life as well. I started reading books not with the aim of scoring marks in the exam but with the aim of acquiring knowledge. Moreover, I have started commanding good respect as a person of great knowledge and no less than a scholar. My relatives and friends seek my guidance when they have to make any crucial decision. The more I read, the more I realize my ignorance which eventually makes me read more. I am convinced that there is no end to knowledge and books are our best companions. I always keep my favourite books with me wherever I go. My hobby of reading books has benefitted me a lot in many ways. First of all, my communication skills have improved a lot and my thinking has become more critical. I am hailed as a good public speaker in my college by the dint of my extensive reading only. Sometimes my name receives a tag of a "bookworm" but I really don't care since I am well aware of the benefits it offers. Though I have gained a lot by reading, I read for the sake of reading. I read because I love to read and I think when you read with a materialistic purpose, it kills the real charm of reading.

Part Three:

Q.1 Are there any negative effects of a person spending too much time on their hobby?
'Hobbies' means the things one likes doing. Every person should have hobbies and should spend time on them. The reason why we pursue hobbies is that they fill us with new vigor and vitality to do our daily chores. But it becomes a matter of worry when one spends all the time on his hobbies and his main duties and daily schedule get disrupted. Wittingly or unwittingly, one gets addict to his hobbies if he pursues them in an uncontrolled manner. Sometimes spending more time on one's

hobby results into unnecessary expenditure if hobbies happen to be expensive.

Q.2 Why do you think people need to have an interest or hobby?
Activities of a person's interest help him unwind and relax himself. Regular and monotonous work whether it happens to be a study or any professional work, makes us feel lethargic and it makes our life mechanical. Everybody needs to be rejuvenated on regular basis in order to do his work with more focus. Indulging in one's hobby is the best way to do so. In addition to filling us with energy, interesting activities work as a stress buster. Philosophically speaking, life is much more than office and family. Spending time regularly for hobbies makes us feel the sense of fulfillment and we feel that we live the life to the fullest.

Q.3 Would you say the amount of free time has changed much in the last fifty years?
The amount of leisure people have nowadays has substantially declined due to many factors. People have to work for longer time in order to meet their ever increasing needs. People in the past had no option but to join the traditional professions which involved no stress and tension. Today life has become more stressful and tensed in the wake of new challenges posed by technological revolution. A person has to devote most of the time of his life for settling down. Undoubtedly we are financially sounder than the people in the past but we badly lack leisure to do the things we like.

Q.4 Do you think hobbies followed by people nowadays are more the reflection of changing fashions and trends than what people actually like?
It is without doubt that fashions and trends change very fast and permeate to the masses in no time thanks to the revolution in the mediums of mass communication. People especially are highly influenced by movies and sports stars therefore they are easily swayed by their likes and dislikes. Further, in order to optimally capitalize on this fad, popular brands hire most famous stars to endorse their products. If it is not less, many multinational companies have entered into fashion industry to cater to the changing needs of market hence it takes very little time for any fashion to become popular. Swanky new bikes, unusual hairstyles, luxurious cars are some of the examples. New trends are no longer an exclusive pastime of an urbane youth since people in rural areas are also seen sporting fashionable things with boast of modernity.

Q.5 What kinds of hobbies people will have in the future?
It is very difficult to make a prediction because our hobbies are dictated by many factors like changing technology and changing trends. As we know that trends change everyday, one can't exactly say what people will like and what they will not, but one thing is for sure that we will be able to see the influence of a global community in future hobbies and interests. Moreover people will love thrilling adventurous activities in order to get relief from stress. We can't deny the fact that favourite pastimes of people will be techno friendly in the wake of technological revolution. If we go by other contradictory belief, people will turn to old and ancient hobbies like outdoor games, traveling and other physically and mentally beneficial activities as people have tasted bitter impacts of technology on health and social lives of people.

Q.6 What factors generally determine one's hobby?
Hobbies change when people grow in the age. Children of poor section of society never get

exposed to expensive sources of entertainment so person's financial background also plays a key role sine rich people are often seen indulging in expensive modes of relaxation like paragliding, scuba diving, boating, car racing. Apart from these things, an environment a person is brought up in and a community a person has grown up in, are also the determining factors.

Interview 37

Part One:

1) What kinds of clothes do you like to wear?

My choice of clothes varies depending upon the occasion and time. Usually I choose jeans and shirt. However I have a great passion for T shirts, I can't wear them everyday as it is considered to be a casual outfit. On traditional occasions, I go for traditional dresses like Salvar and Kamij etc.

2)Do you think clothes are an important part of one's personality?

It is undoubtedly true though clothes do not reveal the real personality of the person which I believe is within. Though many things can be predicted on the basis of the clothes a person wears. Suitable clothes increase the acceptability of the person. For example, a good public speaker will be vehemently criticized if he is dressed in casual outfit i.e. jeans and sleeveless T shirt. A person's sense of cleanliness can also be known by the clothes he wears.

3)Do women wear traditional clothes in your community?

Though women are found to be mostly in traditional dresses, the trend of western outfit is fast catching momentum. As per the tradition, women put on saris after marriage but this has also been defied in recent years and they wear the kind of dresses they like. School and college going girls prefer jeans, T shirts and sometimes Punjabi dresses. However on social occasions and traditional events, women always wear traditional clothes.

4)Some people indulge into exaggerated shopping of expensive clothes. Is it good?

It all depends on individual likes and dislikes. I don't see anything wrong as it doesn't harm the society in any way. A person has complete right to decide what to buy and what not to. People having a passion to follow new trends and fashions usually spend money in an astronomical figure. But one must ensure that it should not be a sickness anyhow and one must keep close watch on his financial resources before indulging in such an exorbitant shopping.

Part Two:

Describe the kid with whom you like to spend more time.
Say.

Who the kid is...
How she/he looks...
What things do you like doing with her/his...

Ans:

I love kids and never miss the opportunity to play with them. There are so many kids around me. Even in my family there are two kids. Both are my brother's children. One is a baby girl named Mahi with whom I love to spend as much time as I get. First of all, I am her as much favourite as she is mine. She looks very cute especially her chubby cheeks make her more beautiful. She is too naughty to be controlled by anybody except me. All the members always take a huge sigh of relief on sunday because it is the only day where they don't have the tension of taking care of her since she is always with on the whole day. She loves to be with me because she knows well that I will fulfil all her demands. She is very stubborn and anyhow manages to get the things she wants. Taking care of her is a formidable task but I still love the job since she loves me a lot. She never takes her dinner if I don't accompany her. Our relation is reciprocal because she never eats any special thing if given by somebody without first giving it to me. She sometimes gets beaten by her mom or dad if she harasses them too much. In such times, I am the only person who takes her side. I like to play with her the games which I used to play in my childhood. Being with her makes me nostalgic and takes me back in my childhood. I can say I am reliving my childhood. I would frankly admit that I really don't like to go home when she is not at home. She has made my life more fulfilling.

Part Three:

Q.1 Why do people think that childhood is the most beautiful period of life?

The main reason behind this belief is that other stages of life are more stressful and full of responsibilities. Children are completely stress free and carefree. They receive lot of love and warmth by their elders. Besides that all the demands of kids are immediately fulfilled and more importantly they don't have to adhere to strict schedule till the time their schooling starts. They have to do nothing except playing, eating and enjoying. However the beauty of childhood is realized when we grow up and it is natural as without going through the burden of responsibilities, no one can know the beauty of childhood.

Q.2 What are some of the problems associated with modern childhood?

I believe early schooling is a big issue and practically speaking it kills the charm and beauty of childhood. Working parents can not pay individualized attention to the upbringing of the kids particularly the food habits and etiquettes or value education. Children today can not enjoy their childhood to the fullest owing to the trend of nuclear family which deprives the kids of the company of the same age kids. In big cities, the security concern also doesn't allow the parents to let their kids go out to play in the nature which eventually leads to indoor sources of entertainment and we have seen the dire consequences of video games and computer games etc. In addition to that, children today are seen suffering from some health hazards like obesity and poor eyesight due to the trend of junk food and hotel food.

Q.3 Do you think children get mature earlier?

Early maturity is a very serious problem nowadays. At a very early age children are exposed to television and internet which robs them of their innocence. Early schooling and ever increasing burden of education don't allow them to play and mingle with other children. They are made to pursue the kind of education which is beyond their psychological abilities. This breeds seriousness and leads to other behavioral disorders. It is often heard that children are involved in some criminal acts. I believe that we are to be blamed as all the parents want their children to grow very fast and unknowingly snatch their childhood which causes early maturity among kids.

Q.4 What is the right age to start schooling according to you?

I am totally against early schooling which has given birth to so many childhood related issues.
I think children should not be shown the school till they finish five years of age. They should not be exposed to books until they gain certain level of maturity. Parents often complain that children do not study but it is bound to happen. If children are forced to study, they will gradually get allergic to books which proves very perilous to their academic career. Children are playful by nature and it is believed that children achieve complete psychological development if they are not burdened and live happily in nature with the kids of same age.

Q.5 How can child's social skill be developed?

Parents can play very crucial role in cultivating social skills among children as children take them as a role model. Another way is encouraging children in the activities which give them a chance to interact with others. For example, children should be made to participate in all the co curricular activities organized in schools. Children should be taken out in social functions as much as possible instead of letting them get stuck on computer games. They should be allowed to mingle with other children which teach them how to socialize. Parents must keep a constant vigil on their behaviour and instruct them if they find anything wrong in the way they deal with others. Children should not talk to their teachers in the same manner as they do with their friends and this should be taught by their parents.

Q.6 Do you think preschoolers should be taught to use the computer ?

I am completely against this idea since I believe there are many more important things to teach them than computer. Sooner or later, they will learn computer as it can be learnt at any stage of life but there are certain things which can be taught at very early stages of life only. For example, more emphasis should be laid on teaching them the right pattern of behaviour and skills of socialization. However I believe they can be introduced to the parts of computer. Teaching them the use of computer is risking making them addict to video games which as we all are aware leads to many complications.

Interview 38

Part One:

1) What place do you most like to visit?

Though I am not so much religious kind of person, I love visiting temples. I usually prefer visiting a very well known temple in my hometown. It is the temple of Goddess Umiya who is coincidentally my community goddess too.

2) How often do you visit this place?

Really speaking, whenever I get leisure, I love to spend some time there. I daily remain present in the temple to attend the evening prayer. The temple, being one of the most visited religious places in the entire country, attracts all my relatives who happen to visit my home. Therefore, I sometimes visit the place upon their insistence.

3)Why do you like it so much?

I personally admire the beauty and cleanliness of the place. The place is the prefect epitome of the proverb that "cleanliness is godliness ". Moreover the food served in the temple's restaurant is extremely delicious and we get a chance to eat in an absolutely divine environment. Honestly confessing, my main aim behind visiting the temple on special occasions is more the food and less the prayer. The place being famous always remains crowded and I like such places.

4) Has it changed very much since you first went there? (In what way?)

Though the original place where the temple is located has not changed much except occasional renovations, other expansions have taken place. A big restaurant, a small amusement park, a well furnished guest house with two hundred odd rooms and ten big dormitories, a nice snacks bar are some of the new facilities which have come up in last five years.

Part Two:

Describe your favourite festival .
Say....
What people do on that day.....
What the festival is...
When it is celebrated...
What you like most about it...

Ans:

India is known as the land of festivals. Nowhere in the world can one find as many festivals as in India. However my favourite festival is Janamastami, the birth anniversary of Lord Krishna. It falls in August but one cannot say exact date as all the festivals follow Sanskrit calendar so the date keeps changing all the time. People celebrate this festival with great zeal and enthusiasm because Lord Krishna is believed to be the superpower that came on the earth to establish a divine order. We have a public holiday on that day and every street and Mohalla is decorated with attractive colours and balloons. Youngsters perform MATAKIFOD in which they form a pyramid and one good looking boy climbs the human pyramid and breaks the pot full of curd and showers it on the people standing and cheering below. Breaking pots and sharing curds was a regular practice in the life of Lord Krishna. Krishna used to do this to feed malnourished children of society. It was a symbolic act to demonstrate that all the resources of the society should be made accessible to all. Nowadays big companies declare exorbitant prizes to those who form the highest pyramid in the concerned city. Youngsters perform street plays to spread the message of Lord Krishna. Krishna was born in the midnight so people get engrossed in wild celebrations till the midnight.

I am a die hard fan of Lord Krishna and find his life very enchanting and captivating. I strongly believe that Lord Krishna is the most misunderstood personality in the whole universe. He was the unique blending of a mystique lover and a shrewd politician which is impossible to find anywhere in the world. He inspires me a lot in all the aspects of life. Krishna appears more an adviser to me than a lord. He has given a best gift to us in the form of the Geeta, which is the lighthouse for all those who want to develop themselves. His life is very unpredictable since he had taken very perplexing decisions in his life. However if observed minutely, the entire life and all events in the life of Lord Krishna seemed to have been directed towards one aim that is to establish a divine order and to destroy the evil rule from the society. I believe that every body should do what Krishna said and not what He did. To celebrate Janamastami in true sense of the word, one should try to bring the spirit of Lord Krishna in one's life.

Part Three:

Q.1 What is the importance of festivals?

All people love festivals since they fill our lives with new fervor and zeal. There is an economic importance associated with the celebrations of festivals. People indulge is excessive shopping to mark the celebrations which help many people earn livelihood. It facilitates the easy circulation of money in society. In addition to this, festivals provide welcome break in our life and invigorate us to concentrate on our work with more energy and focus. Spiritually speaking, festivals make us introspect and peep into our lives to ensure whether we are walking on the right path or not. Evildoers are inspired to come on the right path and good people get motivated to resist the odds and overcome them.

Q.2 Can festival promote tourism? How?

Festivals not only promote tourism but they have the potential to be the biggest source of tourism since all the festivals are very unique in nature and have that edge to attract all those who love and celebrate life. For that to happen, there should be enough advertisement of the festivals across the globe and we must ensure that there should be enough infrastructure for the would-be tourists to make their experience memorable. Festivals which are not religion specific should be shown more aggressively since they hold universal appeal and therefore they should be capitalized on. Religious festivals should not be promoted merely as a celebration but an opportunity to know the concerned nation well.

Q.3 Should one celebrate the festivals of other religions?

This is a welcome idea and should happen to promote unity and secularism. Particularly in democratic nations, it is always desirable that people celebrate all the festivals with great involvement irrespective of their religious identities. Hopefully, it is happening too as we find people of all the religions celebrating Christmas, Diwali and Id etc. But practically speaking, it is very difficult as people sometimes find it hard to associate themselves to other ways of celebrations while on the other hand some liberal minded people enjoy all the festivals. However it is completely up to an individual to decide whether to be a part of other festivals or not but one must respect the festivals of other religions and never criticize them.

Q.4 Are seasons and festivals interconnected?

I think it requires a thorough study or research to establish any relation between festivals and seasons. Religions are celebrated to mark any special religious or spiritual event. However some festivals seem to have been introduced in specific seasons. I have heard somewhere that the kite flying day came into existence to facilitate our maximum exposure to sunlight as the rays of the sun are rich in vitamin D during those days and sunlight is the only source of vitamin D. Though it might be true or a pure coincidence, we cannot generalize that all festivals were introduced considering the factor of season.

Q.5 Do you justify the huge spending by people during festivals?

Indulging into exorbitant shopping on festivals should not be criticized. I think people get good amount of time during festivals to go shopping leisurely. Instead people can shop joyfully. On usual days, we buy things in haste so on festivals shopping itself becomes a part of celebrations. Socially speaking, it gives so many people a chance to earn their bread and butter as sales touch peak during festivals. From economic point of view, festivals work as a catalyst to facilitate the healthy circulation of money in society which is the characteristic of a robust economy.

Q.6 Do you think the way festivals are celebrated nowadays has changed a lot?

Sometimes we feel that today people want festivals as a pretext for lavishness and sometimes immoderation. For them it is not more than one more free day. Real significance of festivals is gradually forgotten and more and more importance is being attached to external pomp and celebrations. Though the observation might be biased and based on individual perception, I believe that people in the past used to understand true significance of festivals and try to change their lives accordingly.

Interview 39

Part One:

1) Do you like to go for shopping?

I like to go for shopping only if there is a real need to go for it. I really do not like to keep roaming in the market or malls just for the sake of it. On festivals and social occasions, I spend lot of time on shopping but I never spend my important time of the day for shopping.

2) Why do people prefer to buy the things from malls?

The main reason is the availability of all the items right from grocery to ornaments under one roof and customers can see variety of the items which help them make better decisions as to what to buy and what not to. Apart from this, the rates in the malls are relatively competitive as they have directly bought the goods from the company. Above all, malls make our shopping experience a memorable one since they have beautiful infrastructure and they cater to other needs of customers as well.

3) Do you see any disadvantages of the same? (buying from malls?)

Sometimes we end up buying the things we actually do not need. Alluring schemes, dazzling infrastructure and aggressive marketing have really made the people buy more and more. Local market and local shop keepers have been rendered redundant since nobody goes to them.

4) Do you think some people are good at buying?

It is true as sometimes we become the victim of cunning practices of shop keepers if we do not have the knowledge of the gimmicks they use to trap customers. Regular buyers are well aware of all these things. In addition to this, some people have good negotiation skills to make a good deal. I personally believe that good shopping skills are the result of an extensive experience of buying the things and sometimes getting fleeced or conned

Part Two:

Describe your favourite mode of exercise.
Say...
Which is the exercise...
Why do you like...
Is it popular among people...

Ans:

With awareness of health on remarkable increase in recent years, people who are conscious about their health are seen doing different kinds of exercises. Most famous are walking, cycling, toing yoga, aerobics and pranayam etc. youngsters obsessed with making good physique attend gymnasiums and take strenuous and exhausting exercise. However I am a great admirer of Yoga, the most ancient mode of exercise. It is widely tried, tested and most trusted form of exercise. Basically Yoga is not an exercise but one of the parts of spiritual practice. It became popular when it came to be known that consistent practice of Yoga helps to remain fit and cure many of the so called incurable diseases. Though physical fitness is the by product of Yoga, it became popular just because of physical advantages. Besides its physical advantages, it is believed that Yoga makes us psychologically healthy if followed with consistency and total involvement. Nowadays medical science has also admitted that Yoga is the most effective exercise as it is the only exercise which directly improves all the systems of the body while other medical practices treat only the symptoms of the diseases. Besides medical benefits, if one does Yoga everyday, his concentration power and overall health improve a lot.

In recent years, Yoga has emerged as the most widely followed mode of exercise due to several reasons. First of all, it costs nothing to its performers as it can be done in any open space and causes everlasting effects on the people. Another reason is that learning Yoga is a matter of one day and Yoga can be done at any time of the day with empty stomach. Other exercises will have negative and harmful effects on the body if done for longer time while yoga is completely harmless. Yoga offers immediate solution to the patients of diabetes and blood pressure and coincidentally the number of the people suffering from these two diseases are continuously rising. For some spiritual seekers, Yoga is a part of their daily rituals and it is popularly believed that Yoga helps one realize God.

Part Three:

Q.1 What is the importance of health in one's life?

Good health is the most important and invaluable asset of the person. Fit and healthy people live happily and can exploit all the available resources well. Even intelligent people cannot bring out their creativity and talent if they are physically unfit. Unhealthy people cannot do their daily work with involvement and remain tense all the time. There is no point in having many materialistic and financial resources if one is unable to use them.

Q.2 How can children be taught the value of health?

It is the responsibility of parents as they are the best people to inculcate good habits among their children. Instilling healthy food habits in children is very important. Children must be aware of what to eat and more importantly what not to eat. It is in vain teaching them the importance of morning walk if parents do not do it. Parents must set an example by doing exercise themselves, by avoiding junk food etc. However society can also play a big role in this regard. Children can be taught the importance of hygiene and cleanliness in schools.

Q.3 Suggest some of the precautions to remain healthy in modern time.

Every person must ensure that he sleeps and eats regularly given that these two are the most dominant factors in ensuring good health. If possible, everybody should at least spare half an hour everyday for exercise which will increase the resistance power. More stress should be laid on home made food only as junk food and hotel food are the main reasons for the worsening standard public health. Regular medical check up also keeps a person updated with his status of health. Most importantly, one must keep himself away from the lethal habits of smoking and drinking alcohol and other drugs.

Q.4 Why do you think people have become more aware of their health today than they used to be in the past?
In the past, people used to be involved in the physically strenuous work hence they never needed any exercise. Besides, environment was clean and there was no pollution. Even food was pure and unadulterated which eventually improves the immunity of the body. So there was no reason why people should be concerned about their health. The picture today is quite disappointing thanks to sedentary lifestyle. Almost all the people after their thirties become victim of at least one lifestyle disease like diabetes, obesity, arthritis, high blood pressure and cardiac disorders. All these factors have contributed to the increased awareness of health.

Q.5 Do you support the huge investment being made in the field of medical infrastructure?
It is always good to have multi-facility hospitals and well equipped research centers. In cases of emergency, accidents and natural disasters, such an investment proves to be a great boon. We must give a credit to enhanced medical facilities for increase in an average life span of people. But still I believe that not enough is being done to educate the people about how to remain fit and disease free. As prevention is always better than cure, more efforts should be made in this direction. It will eventually decrease the need to invest more on infrastructure.

Q.6 Is there any connection between one's life style and his health?
A person's health is, to a great extent, affected by the kind of lifestyle he practices. This was the reason why people were healthy in the past despite the fact that they were voracious eater of high calorie food. All the excess calories got burnt in the tiresome work they used to do. As per the latest surveys, the main cause behinds the deteriorating standard of public health is the sedentary lifestyle. Most of the people today are suffering from lifestyle related diseases. Back pain, obesity, blood pressure, diabetes are some of the diseases which were quite foreign in the past.

Interview 40

Part One:

1) Do you have a large family or a small family ?
I have a large family consisting my parents, my wife, my brother, my sister in law and my little cute daughter, Mahi. My father has been serving in a government sector for last thirty years while I and my wife are involved in our traditional business. My brother works in an MNC. My

little cute daughter Mahi is studying in her pre primary school.

2) Can you tell me something about them?

Being a teacher, my father is very simple but a disciplinarian person. My mother is synonymous with love and generosity since I have never seen as perfect a householder as my mother is. My brother is very intelligent and has done his master's in veterinary science and currently serving in an MNC. My wife is a big support to me in my business of coaching students and agriculture too.

3) How much time do you manage to spend with members of your family?

Honestly speaking, I am far from satisfied with the amount time I spend with my family. My hectic schedule hardly allows me to do so. On an average, I manage to spend two hours in a working day but my weekend is usually dedicated to my family only except some emergency. I really love spending time with my family members as it helps me unwind therefore I prefer being with my family in my leisure time.

4) Do all the family members get on well with one another?

This is the strength of my family. All the members are so committed to the common family good that I really feel proud of all. The secret is that we have very democratic way of running a family since all people get their own sufficient space to fully enjoy the life. I am not exaggerating but whenever there is any occasion where somebody has to make a compromise, there is literally a competition in my family to do so. However, I admit that sometimes there appear some ideological differences between my father and my brother but they are usually sorted out amicably with open minded discussions and I play a role of a mediator.

Part Two:

Describe the most challenging period of your life.
Say...
When you faced that period...
What made it challenging...
Were you able to cope with it...

Ans:

Life is not always a rosy path. It is the blending of bliss and melancholy. I learnt this harsh reality of life at an early stage of life when I was studying in 12th standard. We never know what the destiny has in store for us. I was a student of science stream and doing pretty well in my studies since I wanted to become an engineer from the reputed school of technology. Preparations were in full force for the final board exams but just before two months of an exam, I met with a serious accident. I was returning to my home on my bike after finishing my coaching classes and collided with a car due to the recklessness of the car driver. I fell unconscious and had to be admitted for the surgery on my left leg. Later my father informed me that it would take at least three months to recover and stand on my own feet. I was completely broken down not because my leg was seriously injured but because this event had raised a question mark over my being able to appear for my final exams. I was completely shattered as these two months were the most definitive time in my academic career. Even if I appeared for the exams, I was not in the position to perform well. My parents suggested that I should go for a drop in that year and appear in the exam the next year but they failed to convince me to do so. Though I was completely demoralized, I eventually gathered the courage to take the exams against the wish of my parents. I started my preparations in the hospital and had to tell all the friends and relatives not to come to see me in the hospital as it might make me waste my important time. My family members, particularly my sister helped me get over this trauma and focus more on my studies. I converted a hospital room into a study room and later upon the insistence of my parents, I was discharged before the stipulated date. I thanked the examination centre for having made special arrangement for me to sit on the ground floor. I went to the exam centre and took the support of crutches to walk up to the examination hall. Everybody was watching me with sympathy but was highly appreciative of what I had done. One local newspaper took my interview and published it in the local daily though the language was highly exaggerated and the adjectives used were more than I actually deserve. Though I didn't score as much as I expected and fell short of some marks to get an admission in the school of my choice, this episode of my life has taught me a lot. I learnt to fight and understood the value of determination. A person can do anything however insurmountable the task appears, if he has an unflinching faith in himself. I got admission in another good school of technology and became a civil engineer.

Part Three:

Q .1 What are the different reasons that bring stress?
Life is too uncertain to predict what will be the next thing to face. I think this uncertainty brings stress. Normally reasons of stress vary from individual to individual but there some most common reasons of stress. Financial setbacks, break-up in the relationships, health hazards, unanticipated events like accidents etc are believed to be main reasons which cause stress. However some people are immune to all these things since they believe that life is all about facing uncertain times and challenges. Sometimes there are highly individualized reasons which make people victimized by stress.

Q.2 What are the best ways to deal with stress?
In my opinion, the best way to combat stress is to avoid loneliness and talk to your near and dear ones as much as you can. The more the person is left alone, the more he thinks about the event that has caused stress. Another good and effective way is to switch over the mind to other relaxing activities which will help one get defocused from the setback that has caused the tension. Yoga has also emerged as the biggest stress buster in recent times. If something wrong happens in the life, a person must learn to accept it as a reality of life instead of expecting that it should not have happened. The victim should not exclude himself from the rest of the world and build guilty complex but instead he has to accept the fact that stress is common to all, only reasons vary.

Q.3 What is the role of friendship during tough time?
It is only when people do not have friends, they break down during tough times of life. Though it is a fact that nobody can alter the course of nature and prevent what has happened or what is going to

happen, it is a bigger fact that love and warmth embolden us to overcome the sadness and prepare us to face the situation with more vigor and energy. Moral support is very important in the life and friends are the right people to do so as you cannot share certain facts of life with your other relatives and even your family members. In addition to that, real friends never think of taking any undue advantages of the situation. I also believe that real friendship is tested only during tough times otherwise what is the point in having friends who turn their blind eyes to us when we are under edgy and anxious time.

Q.4 Do you think professional counseling can help in better dealing with stress?

This has come up as a new way of dealing with stressful situations in life. Generally professional counselors are well trained and have the experience as they have come across so many cases which make them better equipped to find out the most realistic solution in each case. They go in the roots of the problem, analyze all the factors and then explore the most effective remedy. Apart from this, they are well aware of the typical kinds of causes which ail the people of a specific class or group or segment. However I believe that solutions offered by professional counselors will not work unless they are well accompanied by the willingness of the affected person and cooperation of family members.

Q.5 Do you think people lead more stressful life today than they used to do in the past?

It is an evident truth as life today has become uncertain, fast and insecure. People have to work harder to meet their ever increasing needs which eventually make them mechanical. Relations have become brittle and pace of the life has accelerated so fast that an individual has to sacrifice a lot just to survive in the stiff competition. Constant threat of insecurity is looming large over people in the wake of newly emerged health hazards, acts of violence in society and increased number of natural disasters. Increasing rate of suicides, other crimes and divorces are the reflection of constantly increasing stress in society. While the situation was completely contrary in the past as people were happier, satisfied with whatever they had and pace of their life was too slow. Their life was totally secure though life was full of hardships.

Q.6 Do you think that overcoming difficulties makes one stronger?

Challenges either make or break a person. The confidence level of an individual is enormously affected by the way he overcomes the crisis because it is often seen that it is only during critical time that a person finds his own worth and manifests the incredible character which he himself was unaware of until the difficulty arose. His self-image improves which endows him with more confidence and readiness to face other ones. History is nothing but the records preserved of the people who triumphantly overcame all challenges of life. The life without problems is not a life at all since they test our character and energy of life. People who overcome the tough time of life usually come out with flying colours since it gives them immense inner power and chance of self discovery.

Interview 41

Part One:

1) Do you prefer to have one particular friend or a group of friends?

My individual opinion favours the idea of having one good friend. It is better to have no friend than to have hundred so called friends. Relationship of friendship is not built just for entertainment or for getting company in parties. What is the point in having so many friends who do not offer an unconditional support in tight corners of life? However I consider the person very fortunate if he gets so many real friends in the life which is extremely difficult.

2) What do you like doing most with friends?

I always appreciate the presence of all my friends in all the times. Most importantly, I love hanging out here and there with friends. Friends make all the moments special. I would not love to visit even the most beautiful place in the world without friends. If friends are with us, they can make any place beautiful and without them any beautiful place appears dull and pale. I like going out for lunch, outing, watching movies, preparing for exams etc. with friends.

3) Do you think it is important to keep in contact with friends you knew as a child?

It is good if somebody succeeds in doing so. It seems difficult to retain all the friends of childhood as all go to different places for studies or other purposes. Some choose other streams of study which compel them to leave the company of childhood friends. But I think we should not leave close friends though we can't remain in touch with all. Old friends should not be forgotten just because we make new friends at different stages of life.

4) Who makes a friend into a good friend?

I think friendship is one of the most misunderstood terms in the world. Friends are many but true friends are a rarity. A good friend is always a good communicator and stands by us even without being asked to do so. He must be a good mind reader and be able to understand our feelings without our verbalizing them. The friends who possess these qualities automatically become good friends.

Part Two:

Describe a museum you have visited.

Say...

When and where you visited it...

What you saw there ...

How you felt about it ...

Ans:

I visited a museum first time in my life when I was studying in a secondary standard in 1999. Our school organized the tour which included a visit to a museum which is located in Jaipur, the capital city of Rajasthan known as Albert hall museum supposedly the oldest one in Rajasthan.

Coincidentally it is the biggest and most famous museum in the country. Positioned amidst the gardens of Ram Niwas Bagh in Jaipur, this museum has an assortment of rare articles on its display including textiles, carpets, paintings, metal and wood crafts, pottery, arms and weapons, flora and fauna of the state, toys, dolls and even an Egyptian mummy that belongs to the Ptolemaic Epoch. It is also known for housing the famous carpet, which portrays the scene of a Persian garden carpet with running water streams that was bought at a dear price from Shah Abbas of Persia, by Mirza Raja Jai Singh. It also puts on show the miniature paintings of a number of sub-schools of Rajasthan, antique jewellery, weapons used in the wars, huge collection of garments worn by royal society and pieces of other ancient artifacts.

Frankly speaking, I am not so fond of visiting museums but I had to go there as it was a part of our itinerary. To be very honest with my experience, I really laughed at myself as for not having visited museum anytime before that. I saw so many such things which really made me stand in awe. All the things seemed to be well preserved by government. I was pleasantly surprised and felt embarrassed too by seeing the number of foreign tourists taking keen interest in our history. The museum is the living testimony of the acme of development our ancestors touched. From that day onwards, I really started taking interest in all the matters regarding history. Museum can play a big role in attracting youngsters and making them realize the glorious history of our country. On that day I understood the importance of a museum and realised that it is not for nothing that people visit them. Museums are the living evidence to prove that the process of development is truly evolutionary. We would not have been able to make such a huge development, had our ancestors not made enough efforts in their times. It is a matter of great regret that since that day, I haven't had any chance to visit any museum again.

Part Three:

Q.1 What purpose do museums serve?

Museums are for the preservation of our valuable heritage. They stand for our glorious past. Moreover they give us an opportunity to sneak a look in the past. Coming generations should know the importance of heritage and pieces preserved in museums are not just material pieces but are priceless treasure of the nation and hence must be preserved in the most dignified way. Things kept in the museum reveal a lot about the life and culture of the different times so they are the symbols of the past.

Q.2 Who visits museums according to you?

People visit museums mostly with a view to knowing something about the life, culture and people in the past. Besides, academicians doing research and people studying history regularly visit museums as it provides vital clues in their studies. Foreigners are deeply fascinated by museums as they love studying various communities and their history so we find them more in museums. But the truth is that most of the visitors are casual visitors who visit museums just because they happen to pass by it or it is a part of the itinerary of their tours.

Q.3 Who do you think enjoys visiting museums more? Elders of youngsters?

Museums should never be considered on a par with other sources of entertainment. I personally think that age is not the factor which makes one interested or uninterested in museums. However we cannot deny the fact that elders usually possess more knowledge of history than youngsters so they find it meaningful to visit museums. Youngsters are seen to be less interested in visiting such places since all of them cannot be expected to be well versed in history. Places having natural beauty and western touch fascinate them more. However I strongly believe that anybody irrespective of the age factor will love visiting museums if he has keen desire to know the history and ancient culture.

Q.4 Some people believe that ancient places should be demolished to make space for commercially useful buildings. Do you agree?

Ancient buildings which have some historical significance are the asset of any nation. They have a huge potential to develop a new source of tourism which will eventually generate good revenue. The value of such buildings cannot be calculated in terms of money. They are the identity of our country and hence should be regularly renovated and preserved with great care. However I am not against the idea of destroying those ancient buildings which have occupied unnecessary space and have no importance at all. No building becomes important just by the virtue of being old.

Q.5 Some people think that museums should be given to private companies for better care and protection. What is your view about it?

The point is worth pondering over as private companies are known to be very professional in their functioning. They will certainly charge money for the entry since they will be motivated by profit factor only but if we think of the positive aspect of this hypothetical situation, they will leave no stone untouched to bring the maximum number of visitors. In addition to that, private companies will invest huge amount of money to maintain museums well in order to attract more people. It will be a win-win situation for government as it will earn huge revenue in the form of tax which will ,in all probability, surpass the income which government generates nowadays by running museums. However I don't support the idea of selling the museums, they should rather be given on the lease basis.

Q.6 Do you think entry in the museums should be free of charge?

Running and maintaining museums involves a huge cost. It requires lot of money to regularly renovate the surroundings. If there is no entry fee, the cost will have to be borne by tax payers. It will be an extra burden on exchequer. Apart from the financial consideration, if there is an entry charge, we can make museums free from any nuisance or at least it will not be like other entertainment places where people come just to gossip and kill their leisure time.

Interview 42

Part One:

1) How do most people travel to work where you live?
I live in the capital city where most of the people are employed in the city itself so they prefer their own private vehicles to commute to their work. People working in far flung areas depend on public transport.

2) What traffic problems are there in your area?
I can boast of living in the city which is completely free from traffic. However we can witness traffic on rare occasions like festivals etc. Being a capital city, national level political leaders and other celebrities often visit my city. It also causes traffic sometimes.

3) How do traffic problems affect you?
Traffic irritates me a lot since I am not used to facing much traffic in my city. But whenever I am stuck in the traffic situation, I have to waste a lot of time and get tired. I really can't concentrate on my work after getting stranded in traffic.

4) How would you reduce the traffic problems in your area?
Though traffic in my city is a rare occurrence, I believe it too can be avoided by implementing some measures. As traffic occurs less, we do not have more and advanced traffic control mechanisms in place. If traffic is electronically monitored, we can nab the offenders easily. Traffic police must remain present irrespective of the fact that traffic occurs or not.

Part Two:

Describe the biography or autobiography you have read.
Say...
Whose biography\autobiography was it...
Why you read it...
Why you liked it...
Anything special about it...

Ans:
Though I very honestly admit that I am not a voracious reader, I love reading widely popular books. I have read only one auto biography in my lifetime that is “My experiments with truth “written by Gandhi, father of the nation who is fondly called “Bapu”. I am more fascinated by the lives of movie stars and cricketers but I read this book because it was my birthday gift. Before I read the book, I knew many things about this book. I was told by my father that it is one of the most widely read autobiographies in the whole world. It has not only influenced common men but many globally acclaimed celebrities have also been moved by this book. The only reason why I started reading this book was that I wanted to please my father because it was gifted to me by none other than him.

Let me be honest here and say that once I began reading it, I couldn't help myself but to read ahead and ahead. On one day, I finished above fifty pages at one go. I have never found and perhaps will never find such a transparent person as Gandhi was. The prefix "Mahatma" very well suits him. I don't know who conferred him with this attribute but I salute him as this attribute would never have found as deserving person as Gandhi was. Most of the autobiographies are written for self propaganda but Gandhi had written it for self admission. He had revealed so many secrets of his life in the book without caring about his ever increasing reputation at the time of release. This book has inspired me a lot since I saw me in Gandhi. Gandhi was as common man as we are. He was not born with special powers. Whatever he achieved in his life is only by the dint of his honesty and unconditional adherence to the principles. After reading the whole book, I realized that only Gandhi can inspire common people because we can associate ourselves with him. Other personalities are too great and glittering to be imitated by common men. I asked myself a question, "If Gandhi can, why can't I?"

Since that day, I have become a great admired and follower of Gandhi and I got a chance to know him in his own words. The book is written in such an eloquent language that you will never feel that you are reading it, rather you will feel that Gandhi is talking to you. It has been translated in almost all the major languages of the world. This birthday gift will always remain special to me.

Part Three:

Q.1 Why do people read biographies and autobiographies?

People have always been dazzled and fascinated by the lives of great people. Extra ordinary feats achieved by some people make them heroes in the eyes of millions of people. This awe and adulation for those heroes make them take keen interest in their lives. Besides this factor, people read biographies or autobiographies to get motivated. Greatness is never accidental.

Great people always have to make huge sacrifices and overcome many odds in the life in order to succeed. Sometimes we get solutions to our problems from the lives of great people. In order to understand any personality, it is important to know about his social and educational background and more importantly the circumstances which shaped his personality. Sometimes controversial people also arouse interest in their lives.

Q.2 What do you think makes a great or a well known person write his biography?

The objective varies from person to person but most commonly, the purpose is huge fan following. That is the reason why popular people do this. It is an attempt to satisfy the curiosity of their followers who are always inquisitive to know more and more about them. Some really great personalities want their life to be a lighthouse for others and really believe that their life can prove to be a motivation for millions. This makes them pen down their autobiographies though they are not hungry for fame. Some controversial people use their autobiographies as a publicity tool by concocting some more controversial stories. Politicians tend to do so in order to make people aware of the political realities prevailing in the country and justify the decisions they had taken when they were at the helm of affairs.

Q.3 How does reading biographies differ from reading auto biographies?

Auto biography tends to be more real and reliable as it is written by the person himself and the writer is the right person what has happened in his life. In the case of biography, writer's individuality is bound to have an impact in justifying the person being written about. Writers will always evaluate the episodes from their perspectives and perceptions. Nobody else can write what others have felt or gone through in certain episodes of life in their behalf. However convincing the language might be in a biography, it will always lag behind in communication. But there is a positive aspect of biographies that readers are likely to get more objective information from biographies since writers sometimes tend to justify their decisions in autobiographies.

Q.4 Do you think biographies are always exaggerated?

It largely depends upon who the writer is. If it is written by the admirer or a follower of the concerned personality, it is bound to be exaggerated. The writer can never see the things as they are and will try to paint everything with good colours since he is deeply influenced by the person he is writing about. If the writer is a dispassionate and writes objectively, everything will be written in an unbiased and an impartial manner. However writer's individuality will always affect the intelligibility of the content but the biography will be far from being overstated.

Q.5 Some biographies have been made into films. Which is better the written form or the film version?

Film making on real life characters is a completely different thing. Films can not be expected to strictly stick to the original story. There are bound to be the artistic requirements which eventually force the film makers to make changes to the original plot. Film making is completely a creative and imaginative job hence it calls for modifications to fit the plot and to embellish the story. So I personally think that films can not justify any character in an unbiased and a fair manner. Another factor is that films can not reveal all the details in an elaborated manner due to time limitation which books can do well. Though books are also not free from the allegations of bias and prejudice but they are bit more reliable and closer to reality than films. Despite all these things, films are more preferred than books since it takes less time to watch a movie than to read a book.

Q.6 Do you think biographies of national heroes help the young?

I believe I will not merely help them but it's a need of an hour. Nowadays younger generation seems to be completely oblivious of the sacrifices made by the national heroes. Their lives offer a lot to learn and breed the feeling of patriotism. They can have better ideals in life. They must know that the acts of bravery and courage they see in movies are possible too in real life. The heroic acts of some of the national heroes are far more motivating than any film actor can depict in his wildest dreams. Young people will be aware of the contribution made by such heroes and will try to imitate them.

Interview 43

Part One:

1) Do you enjoy dancing? (Why/ Why not?)

I like to dance but I actually don't know how to dance well. My dance can please me but it will not please the spectators. I mean I can't dance well. I wish I had developed this skill. I enjoy doing it a lot because I take it as an exercise. When we dance, we perspire a lot and it requires lot of energy and agility to dance well. I think I am a good dancer when I dance alone but my inability to dance well holds me back.

2) Has anyone ever taught you to dance? (why/why not?)

I have never made an attempt to learn to dance under professional guidance. I mean I haven't gone through any formal training to learn dance. When I was studying in my school, I participated in a dance competition and my school teacher taught me how to dance. She was an excellent dancer and taught me that dance is not about just taking steps but it is an expression of the song and one has to lose himself to bring mesmerizing effects in one's dance.

3) Tell me about any traditional dancing in your country.

We have many forms of classical dance in our country and the most popular among them is Bharat Natyam. But Garaba is the most popular one among all. It is also called "street dance" or "dandiya". It is particularly performed during Navarattri, a nine-night festival. Garaba is performed in group in synchronized actions by all the participants.

4) Do you think that traditional dancing will be popular in future? (why/why not)

Traditional dance has stood the test of time and competition from other forms of dance like rock, pop dance etc. it has not only survived but has increased in popularity. For example, Navaratri is being celebrated with an ever rising zeal and pomp. On the contrary, coming generations will be more attracted towards traditional dance in order to remain connected with their culture.

Part Two:

A tradition you like to preserve.
Say..
Which one...
What is its importance...
Why do you like it...

Ans:

Indian being a traditional country, we follow so many traditions in our daily life. Some traditions seem to be outdated and hold no value in modern time. Every tradition was initiated keeping in the view the social and religious circumstances of that time. There is no point in continuing them as social circumstances have completely changed. Though I believe most of the religious and social traditions are incongruous, some traditions are eternally beneficial to society.

I am an open advocate of some traditions and believe that they must be preserved at any cost. Some people are iconoclast and keep criticizing traditions for the sake of doing so. There is an underlying philosophy behind all the traditions and that needs to be understood in order to understand the importance of any tradition. In our country, there is a tradition of worshipping God before doing or starting a new work. It prevails everywhere in the country. This tradition gives a touch of auspiciousness and religiousness to whatever we do. In addition to that, it is a gesture which states that there is nothing beyond and above the will of the Almighty. It is because of His blessings that we humans can breathe and exist. This is an expression of gratitude towards the creator of the universe. Moreover it makes us humble enough to admit that we are not all omnipotent. Giving credit to God for anything new is a sign of spiritual development. However there is a fear factor inherent within this tradition. People believe that nothing untoward will happen if we remember God in the beginning. God will keep the whole work or event free from any evil and bad consequences. I have deep sense of gratitude towards God and firmly believe that human effort will not bring success if it is not accompanied by the blessings of Almighty. I start my day with a prayer. Not only this, all my important tasks are preceded by a prayer. It fills me with positive energy and optimism. I have noticed that even fear of failure also fails to deter your efforts if you have an unflinching faith in Almighty.

Part Three:

Q.1 Why do some people continue to follow traditions even in the modern time?
Traditions keep people connected with their culture. They give a sense of security and an identity to the followers. All the traditions have some spiritual significance or historical importance associated with them. I think the best way to socialize is to follow the traditions as they give a chance to mingle and mix with people. On the contrary, people adhere more strictly to traditions, since people feel that their culture is threatened by globalization and the best way to save the culture is to keep its traditions alive and intact hence traditions are followed unquestionably.

Q.2 Do you think young people do not like to follow traditions?
In the wake of emerging global culture and increasing exposure to western societies, many young people have started questioning the significance of their traditions. Educated minds are not ready to accept anything without critically evaluating it. Any tradition must stand on the touchstone of intellect in order to survive. This change is good and must be welcome with open arms. It is often seen that people condemn traditions to appear sophisticated and well-educated. They are dazzled by western culture and under undue influence of it. Nobody becomes well educated just because he abhors his traditions. This is not appreciable at all and must be strongly discouraged.

Q.3 Does anything become important just because a tradition is associated with it?
It is not so but keeping larger good of society in mind, it is good to follow traditions because people will not dare to violate them. When any activity becomes a part of wide spread social behaviour, it

has to have something crucial in it. Though traditions are nothing but important activities incorporated in social behaviour for the sustained good of society, I believe some traditions get useless and irrelevant with the passage of time and hence need to be discarded. On the other hand, some traditions that are in the interest of people in general have survived all odds. The best example is the success of the institution of marriage. In our country, marriage is considered to be an inviolable and sacred phenomenon just because some traditions are associated with it.

Q.4 Do you think future generations will follow traditions?

It makes me quite skeptical. Even today some traditions have already been forgotten and mocked. The more people become educated and come in contact with the external world through media and internet, the more they get allergic to their native culture and traditions. The life of future generation will be dominated by technology. Social networking sites are fast emerging as the most preferred mode of communication which has defied geographical and cultural boundaries and exposed people to the whole world. In future, lifestyles will not allow people to spare time for such things. People will not only forget but will make mockery of traditions.

Q.5 Can you mention some occasions which have certain customs linked with them?

In our country, every social occasion is connected with some customs. Even to give a name to a newly born baby, there is a custom called nomenclature. Final rites are conducted for the

eternal peace of the departed soul. Together there are sixteen occasions which have to be strictly performed with traditional ceremonies. Failing to do so invites social wrath and it is considered no less than a blasphemy. More specifically, we see more customs and rituals are carried out during marriages and funerals.

Q.6 Do you think traditions cause divide between villages and cities?

I agree that more traditions have been preserved in villages and the lifestyle is also to certain level more orthodox and conventional. People in villages have less exposure to the outer world since technology is yet to make a way into rural culture. Contrary to that, people in cities are more open minded and are influenced by changing trends in the world which eventually make them analytical and critical in thinking. They discard what appears outdated and irrelevant. They don't feel hesitant in accepting the beneficial thing even if these things belong to other culture. I still believe that this is not the only thing which makes villages different from cities.

Interview 44

Part One:

1) How important are the clothes to you? (Why/Why not?)

Clothes hold value for all, but for me the case is different. I have a great passion for clothes and really love wearing different brands and like to experiment with changing trends and fashions. I spend a lot on clothes which my father doesn't approve. I think clothes make you modern and give you the touch of sophistication.

2) What kinds of clothes do you dislike? (Why/Why not?)

I hate extremely traditionally clothes. I personally feel that we get thrown out of the mainstream if we wear highly traditional clothes. Besides this, I don't like any cloth however expensive or attractive it might be, if it is made from any other fabric except cotton.

3) How different are the clothes you wear now from those you wore 10 years ago?

Ten years ago, I used to be a school going boy and left with no choice but to wear the school uniform. I guess I might not have cultivated the sense of fashion at that time. Even casual clothes were of my parents' selection. Nowadays, I have developed a great fashion sense and have a penchant for clothes. I can't allow anybody to select my clothes on my behalf. I like jeans of various patterns and branded t-shirts. On good occasions, I like to put on formal pairs of pants and shirts.

4) What do you think the clothes we wear say about us?

Contrary to popular belief, I hold the view that clothes hardly reveal anything about the personality of the wearer. It is all about the choice of colour, pattern and fabric. Yes, clothes certainly speak a lot about the person's taste of fashion and choice of colours. People wearing unsuitable clothes can be said to lack the sense of aesthetics. If clothes are any indication of what the people actually are, politicians must be the people of highest integrity and credibility.

Part Two:

Describe your favourite sportsman.
Say...
Who he is...
His achievements...
Why you like him...

Ans:

Being a die hard fan of cricket, I admire so many cricketers across the world. I am a good reader of the game so only cricketers of exquisite skills and technique can impress me. However my all time favourite cricketer is Mahendra Sing Dhoni who is always criticized for lacking techniques to play some shots. His achievements are innumerable and he is considered to be the most successful captain and wicket-keeper batsman of Indian cricket team. Under his able leadership, India won the ICC cricket world cup in 2011 after twenty eight years. He is the second captain after Kapil Dev to have brought this coveted trophy to India. Not only this, he led the team to victory in twenty-twenty world cup first time when the tournament was introduced. As this is not enough, India's test team reached the top on the ICC cricket ranking after thirty five years. He has proven himself in all the three formats of cricket. His performance as a cricketer and wicket keeper is also fabulous. He is well known for playing under critical circumstances when the team badly needs runs. His method of playing unconventional shots has been admired by some and criticized by some. He has many a time bailed out the team from tough times. His knock in the world cup final has immortalized him in the world cricket. I appreciate Dhoni more as a leader than as a player. One can find many good cricketers in the world cricket who can be even a better player than him but finding an able leader like him is next to impossible task. He is popularly known as "captain cool". He keeps his cool under any situation. His career as a captain is completely uncontroversial, which is really a commendable task in the sub continent like India where cricket is no less than a religion. The way he commands respect from seniors and new players is really appreciable. More importantly, the way he manages his relations with BCCI, selection committee, his colleagues, fans and media speaks volumes of his being a good communicator. One rarely finds him losing temper or overreacting either on or off the ground. Sometimes I feel that he is born to uplift Indian cricket and true to his credit, Indian cricket has really blossomed under his leadership. He is the highest paid cricketer for brand endorsement.

Part Three:

Q.1 Sportsmen are paid more than other important professionals like doctors, engineers, artists. Is it fair?

I believe that other professions are equally important and beneficial for society but I am in complete favour of sportsmen being paid heftily. They carry challenging responsibility to glorify the name of the nation on their shoulders and there is a continuous stress to do well at the highest level. In addition to that, their career lasts for a shorter span and that too is vulnerable while in other professions, people keep working even in the twilight of their lives. Once their performance drops a little, they are thrown out of the team. Sometimes tough competition takes a toll on their body. Not only this, the threat of untoward injury constantly looms large over them. Considering all these factors, I can say they deserve more than what they are actually getting.

Q.2 Today sportsmen are hero worshipped like film stars. Is it fair?

Nowadays sportsmen receive tremendous media attention. This is a result of increased public interest in the life of sportsmen. I don't think it is deplorable. If movie stars enjoy huge fan following just by entertaining them, sportsmen play a far bigger role than them. Spirit of nationalism is always associated with sports so they have to remain industrious and alert. Sportsmen do on the ground, what actors do on screen. They are the heroes in the real life because their small error can cost the nation dearly. So I think it is not only fair but desirable too.

Q.3 Do you think big prize money involved in sports has killed sportsmanship?

I think it has affected the very purpose of the sport. Sportsmen today are accused of being more concerned with their vested interests than the interest of the nation. Sports have been commercialized nowadays and huge money involved in it has distracted the focus of sportsmen. They really perform well but the motive behind this performance is to earn name and money rather than to win the match or glorify the name of the nation. Patriotism was the driving force behind making the decision of joining any sport but nowadays money is the sole guiding force. Money has destroyed the real spirit of the game. That is the reason why politicians are showing keen interest in controlling sports federations.

Q.4 Would you agree that sports play a big role in easing international tension?
Sports not only ease international tensions but improve the relationship. People to people contact is the best confidence building measure if there is a conflicting relation between two countries and sports can serve to be the best medium to initiate the public interaction. People talk to one another, congratulate their counterparts even after losing the match, and get involved in chatting when they face each other during the matches. These friendly gestures are very important for both the concerned nations which will eventually pave the way for more constructive dialogues. Only sports can create conducive environment for dialogues. However we cannot ignore the danger involved in establishing sports link between two conflicting countries. In place of easing, it can intensify the tension. The suppressed animosity towards each other finds expression during the match if the patriotic sentiments of any group are hurt by the other group either by raising inflammatory slogans or placards. It can incite violence.

Q.5 What are the values a child learns while playing a game?
Undoubtedly a child improves his health and fitness. Apart from this physiological gain, sports teach so many values. The most important is sportsman spirit. On field hostility must be forgotten after the game is over. The decision taken by an umpire must be welcomed with a smiling face however unacceptable it may appear. Sports should be played without fear and favour. One must learn to keep the face smiling after defeat and congratulate the winning team or player. Child learns to make decisions on his own. Moreover his leadership qualities get the boost if he is leading the team. Fighting spirit and the attitude of "never-give- up" are very important values of life which can be cultivated by sports.

Q.6 Are you satisfied with the amount of importance being given to sports in modern education system?
Modern education system seems to be overburdened with so many academic subjects. To make students skilled and eligible enough to survive the tough competition in the world, more and more academic subjects are being accommodated in the education system and to make the room for academic subjects, important subjects like sports are being sacrificed. I firmly believe that sports must be given considerable space in a curriculum since they relieve the stress of the study and make them physically fit. Sports should be compulsorily taught to all students. A school without a playground cannot be worthy to be called a school.

Interview 45

Part One:

1) Do you like to visit natural places? (Why/Why not?)

Whenever I get free time, I visit the places which have abundance of natural beauty. Such places give me deep solace and tranquility of mind. Most importantly, I can get some time to talk to myself. Nature heals our mind as we forget our tension and worries in the lap of nature.

2) With whom do you like to visit them?

I prefer visiting such places alone. Going there with friends or family members kills its basic purpose because I go there for contemplation and reflection. I get an opportunity for introspection and to make better planning of future. However I certainly love the company of my friends, if I go to the cinema, shopping and for outing.

3) Is there any such place near your hometown?

A very famous hill station named Mount Abu is not so far from my hometown. It is nearly hundred kilometers and requires just two hours to travel by car. It is really a fascinating and enthralling place. It is not only rich with trees and rocks but a shelter of many wild animals too.

4) On what occasions do you like to visit such places?

Such beautiful places remain jam-packed during vacations and festivals. So I prefer another time because I don't like cacophonous and crowded places. I don't go there on specific occasions but whenever I feel like needing a break or energy, I go there.

Part Two:

Your favourite female icon.
Say...
Who the person is...
Her achievements...
Why she is your favourite...

Ans:

There isn't any field or sector untouched by women. They have made a remarkable progress in all the fields. I am inspired by the famous social activist Kiran Bedi. She used to be a police officer and she is the first woman police officer in independent India. I don't know more about her personal and family background. In her professional life, she was enjoying the status of being an honest and incorruptible police officer. Since she retired, she has continued to serve the nation by forming her own N.G.O and by being a part of many social movements. She got many offers from the corporate world to provide her services thanks to her impeccable track record but she happily turned them down as she wanted to be of some help to society.

I hold her in high regards because she is a person of the highest commitment and integrity. In recent time, she is in the news for her active role in leading a civil society movement to pressurize the government to enact an anti corruption ombudsmen named Lokpal bill. Government in power tried its level best to defame her and crush the movement but she brilliantly answered all the questions raised by the government on the credibility of the agitation. This fighting spirit of hers has made her an icon in the eyes of millions. She is a selfless social worker committed to the welfare of society. Many times she has been put behind bars for sitting on fast or leading a campaign alleging that she is causing an unrest and commotion in the society. These odds have, instead of deterring her spirit, have strengthened her resolve to fight and give this country a strong anti corruption law. Her fight doesn't end here; she works for the larger cause of generating political awareness among the people and of correcting the flaws in the parliamentary democracy. She has set a new standard for women. She is an apt and ideal example of what women can do. She has defied the age old belief that woman cannot be a good leader.

Part Three:

Q.1 Do you think the role of women has been changing in society?
Women have been playing a great role as a caretaker of society for ages and they have also proven that if they are given a chance and opportunity, they can successfully justify any given role. Education standard among the women nowadays is far better than men. The contribution of women in modern world can never be overlooked. Apart from the role of generating income for their families, women nowadays are seen being active players in many social causes. They have proven their worth in politics and social services too. The most noticeable thing is that they have achieved all these milestones without sacrificing their primary roles. Women are no longer mute spectators witnessing the change but they are causing the change.

Q.2 What kinds of problems are faced by women nowadays?
A woman sometimes becomes the victim of domestic violence if she is not able to bear a child or a male child. Physical and mental harassment in public places and even in the homes is a big issue. Mostly in all the family disputes, women are always at the receiving end. The biggest crime in my opinion is not to allow a female child to breathe on the earth. I mean people obsessed with having a male child indulge into the practice of sex determination and if the child happens to be girl, they go for female feticide. Physical abuse and rapes are also inhuman acts committed against women. Fortunately the cases of dowry are on decline thanks to improving educational standards.

Q.3 Are you in favour of reservation for women in jobs?
I am strictly against the idea of reservation just to bring them on a par with men or for their empowerment. Jobs should be given on the basis of merit only. However I believe that they should be given more opportunities in education. In addition to that, subsidies can be made available for the education of girls especially from financially poor sections of society. Reservation will breed partiality and inefficiency. Rather efforts should be made to make them eligible enough to compete with the best.

Q.4 Do you think the existing laws are not strict enough to ensure the safety of women?

Laws are always strict but what matters more is implementation of the laws. Even some laws are tilted in favour of women. I believe that existing laws are enough to ensure their safety but it is the lengthy judicial process which doesn't allow the law from taking its own course. I believe that there should be fast tract courts to deal with the cases concerning the safety of women. As it is rightly said that justice delayed is justice denied. Fast delivery of justice can only do something good in this regard. However, I am of the view that capital punishment should be meted out to rapists so that they do not perpetrate this heinous crime again. People committing such heinous crimes deserve no less than that.

Q.5 Do you think women are better at certain jobs?

Their nature works in their favour. Women are caring and emotional by nature. Commitment and dedication are the part of their being. These traits of their personality are an asset in service industry. They have traditionally acquired the skills of management since house keeping is the job not less demanding than managing a company. All these skills make them fit enough for the job which involves services. For example women can definitely prove to be better in the hospitality, medical and teaching professions.

Q.6 Do you think there are any disadvantages if women work outside?

This can prove either a great boon or a curse. It largely depends upon the woman concerned. If the woman does it at the cost of her fundamental roles like the roles of a mother or a wife, it is certainly deplorable. In the race of being manlike, women must not lose her charm of womanhood. But sometimes the fact that she works outside makes her a good mother. She will not only be a pampering mom but an adviser too for her children. She will be a great financial support to her husband. A working woman is a social reality which cannot be stopped and should not be stopped either. More critical evaluation is required to ascertain its larger consequences on society.

Interview 46

Part One:

1) How do you keep yourself fit?

I believe that food plays a very important role in keeping us fit. I eat only home made food. If I occasionally happen to eat outside, I eat my regular food only and that too in less proportion. I seldom take oily snacks. I don't take exercise everyday but I play cricket. I drink a lot of water and other fluids and I think it is good for the body.

2) What do the people of your community do for their health and fitness?

It varies from people to people but there are certain things people do, like Yoga. Many people attend their morning walk on regular basis. Laughing clubs are not so popular but young people go to gymnasiums to keep themselves in shape.

3) Do you think your being fit helps you in other aspects of life?

It not only helps but plays a key role in my life. I can do any work with energy and concentration only by the dint of my fitness and sound health. Moreover, it makes me charming and attractive since my face always reflects enthusiasm and confidence.

4) Who is the healthiest in your family in your view?

My father is my ideal in fitness. Even at the age of fifty two, he has an enviable fitness. Credit goes to his habit of taking exercise everyday unfailingly. He is very particular in his diet. His energy and stamina is really commendable. He is free from any disease and he is the adviser of all the family members in the matters of health.

Part Two:

Speak about your favourite vehicle.
Say...
Which one...
What do you know about it...
How popular it is...
Why you like it...

Ans:

Since my school days, I have had a great passion for automobiles, particularly cars. I read automobile magazines and watch all news in regard to new arrivals in the market. I don't think there is any famous car which is not in my knowledge. I specifically admire German technology in automobile sector but my favourite car is Captiva. It is manufactured by Chevrolet the segment of General Motors. It is the biggest car manufacturer in the world. Captiva is one of the best sellers in S.U.V segment. It has all the good features which any automobile expert can list out on the page. The main one which has made it very popular is powerful 2000 cc engine and captivating look. It contains all the other common features like electronically operated windows and electrical power steering etc. Above all, it has tremendous safety provisions like dual air bags, radial wheels, reverse sensor etc.

It is a very popular car and has caught the imagination of car lovers. People who want to be thrilled by driving are more attracted by this car. In addition to this, it doesn't have a typical sports look so many professional people too buy this car due to its good safety features. It has become a symbol of status. If somebody tries to find the car of the same features in other companies like Nissan, Volkswagen, Mercedes, BMW or Audi, the car will cost him very dearly. The beauty of this car is that it offers all the facilities which only famous luxury cars of the world can provide and that too at the affordable price which can fit the budget of the upper middle class. I like it for the simple reason that it is my dream car. It suits my personality and I believe that I will be able to buy it at one stage of my life considering its competitive cost. I am charmed by its look so much that I have taken the test drive even without any planning to buy it. Anybody having this car can make me feel jealous only.

Part Three:

Q.1 Why do you think people buy cars nowadays?

The main reason is the increasing mobility of life. People cannot afford to waste time in traveling. Second reason is safety since we can comfortably travel in all the seasons. Moreover increasing purchasing ability of middle class has led to a dramatic rise in car selling. Unfortunately people sometimes indulge in showing off. Despite being financially unable to buy it, they take loans and buy cars just to show off their status. Easy availability of loans has added fuel to the flame. Besides all these factors, aggressive marketing and irresistibly tempting selling tactics by automobile companies also lure people into buying cars.

Q.2 Do you think increasing car sale causes air pollution?

It is an evident fact that increasing number of cars on the road is the major factor contributing to air pollution. The more cars are, the more consumption is. Government can ban the industries emitting poisonous gases and it can be done by framing stringent laws but how can car selling be curbed? Car selling continues unabated despite levying heavy taxes on the sale of an automobile. As it is a well known fact that cars are causing the highest consumption of fuels, car selling needs to be curbed.

Q.3 How can a city or town restrict the use of private vehicles?

This welcome change is difficult to achieve but can be achieved by taking some pragmatic measures. First of all, public transport should be made more competitive and must be run professionally. More facilities, good frequency, well maintained vehicles, cleanliness and regularity are some of the factors which can attract daily commuters towards public transport. Traveling by private vehicles is certainly an expensive affair, but people do so out of helplessness as they do not have any reliable source of traveling. If public transport can assure people of its efficiency and reliability, people will definitely start using it.

Q.4 How can we make our roads safer places to drive?

First of all, I would like to blame the wide spread corruption in government sector for poorly constructed roads. If good material was used to make roads, we could avert many accidents. Another factor is that no enough precautions are taken to remove the water during rainy season specifically in low lying areas. The stagnation of water for prolonged period damages the roads. I also believe that we should make enough provisions to protect the roads. Roads flanked by rows of trees are better protected.

Q.5 Do you think traffic rules need to be made more stringent to control traffic?

I think the need of hour is education and awareness. The existing laws are more than enough to effectively combat the menace of traffic. The broad and major issue is different. People are often completely unaware of traffic norms and when they are caught, set themselves free by offering bribe. This needs to be changed. I think a driving licence should not be issued without thoroughly assessing the knowledge of an applicant. Apart from this, authorities must ensure proper implementation of traffic rules and stop traffic cops from indulging into any malpractice.

Q.6 What things should a person bear in mind while driving to ensure safety?

The main thing is mental alertness and focus. Most of the accidents on road occur by individual carelessness. Reckless driving, driving under the influence, use of a mobile, music system at high volume are such things which must be avoided without saying. One must put on safety measures like helmet or seatbelt before one turns the vehicle on. Knowledge of road rules is vital. Apart from these factors, vehicles of daily use must be maintained on time to time basis to ensure their smooth functioning.

Interview 47

Part One:

1) Do you like watching movies? (Why / Why not)

I am a regular cinema goer. I like watching all kinds of movies very much. I believe movies not only give us an entertainment but they educate us as well. Besides, movies are the best medium to know the changing trends of the world. I think watching a movie is as good an art as making a movie.

2) Which kinds of movies do you like to watch very much?

I specifically love to watch the movies which are based on real life stories or characters, for the simple reason of motivation. This is the best way to revive historical characters. I also admire art house movies. They have something to say and one needs to have that aesthetic sense to understand such movies.

3) Which kinds of movies achieve more success nowadays?

People prefer to watch comedy movies more since they give a chance to relax and laugh. I believe life has become more stressful nowadays and people seldom get the chance to laugh. That is the reason why comedy movies are seen to be ruling the box office despite having very silly and idiotic stories. Very inspirational and message yielding movies also taste a good deal of success. Love stories and romantic movies no longer seem to be the flavour of the season.

4) Do you think you can act well?

I used to act really well during my school days. I had won so many prizes for my wonderful acting in the public functions. Nowadays I can't say that I can act because after I left my school, I have never participated in any programme. I think I can act; the only thing is that I have to practise extensively.

Part Two:

Describe an occasion where you had a difference of opinion with any family member
Say...
What was the matter...
How you resolved ...
Who was the member...
What you learnt...

Ans:

In most of the cases, my father, being the head of the family makes all the decisions pertaining to family matters. However we all the members of the family enjoy the individual freedom at least to make the decisions on our own in our individual life. Once my father decided to buy a new home as our previous house was bit smaller. There was a discussion in the family as to in which area the house should be bought. My father asked for the opinion of all the members. All the family members agreed upon the choice of my father except me. I wanted to have our own house in the area of my choice because my all the friends were living in that area. I was too adamant to give in since my father had promised me in the past that he would buy the new home in the location of my preference. I even reminded him of his promise. My father tried his level best to convince me to approve his choice and even expressed his regret for not having been able to keep his word. All my family members also joined my father in persuading me to happily respect the choice of the family. Being the youngest person of the family, I am very stubborn by nature and all my needs had been fulfilled.On that day in the night, my father called me in his room and explained all the reasons in detail why he couldn't buy the house in the area of my choice. I understood the situation of my father. I did not know that the cost of real estate was too high to buy a house for us in the area that I was insisting on. I really felt sorry and apologized to my father. I really thanked my father for taking me in the confidence rather than imposing his decision on me. In the morning, I told all the family members that I was more than happy to go with their choice. Everybody breathed the sigh of relief. The matter was resolved amicably but I learnt many things from that episode of my life. First of all, we must not express our opinion without understanding all the aspects of the matter. One more thing I learnt from my father that the best way to resolve any issue is dialogue and communication. My father was in complete right to have totally disregarded my opinion and gone ahead with his decision. I realized the importance of communication within family members on that day.

Part Three:

Q.1 What is the importance of family in an individual's life?

It is the institution of family which separates man from the animal world. An individual feels emotional security in family because we never feel alone. It is only because of family support that man can live happily. Healthy family relations always affect one's mental and emotional well being. Sense of belonging to family plays an important role in everybody's life. It is because of family that a person learns how to behave and adapt to others. A person learns to live for others. It is the institution of family which teaches us to look beyond and above personal interests.

Q.2 Do you think family unit is gradually losing its significance?

As people have come under great influence of various cultures due to globalization, fast growing media and the internet, the paradigms are changing too with equal pace. Modern youngsters speak the language of individual freedom. They don't want their privacy to be attacked by family consideration. The term “compromise” is misinterpreted and being considered as an interference into one's life. Excessive importance is being given to one's individuality which has resulted into the degradation of family unit.

Q.3 What are the advantages of living in a joint family?

I think we are gradually heading toward the universal trend of nuclear family and hence tend to forget the advantages that joint family offers. First of all, sense of security is felt only in joint family. Guidance of parents helps us make better decisions. The biggest advantage in my opinion is the upbringing of children. Children receive a lot of love and care by elders and other members of family. In case of financial crisis, family can survive on the basis of other members' income. In adverse times, all the members can together combat with the circumstances. United, we rise.

Divided, we fall.

Q.4 What causes family divide?

Reasons can be so many. In the times of competitive world, some people have to go far from their natives to get better employment. In such cases, some members have to accompany the concerned person and settle in other regions. Sometimes extreme differences of opinion between younger generation and elders too cause divide. Particularly when the gap is irreconcilable, going separate seems to be the only solution. Intolerance and inability to adapt to others by some members of family are also the main factors nowadays.

Q.5 Why do you think some people voluntarily decide to accept nuclear family?

It is because they do not get sufficient space in joint family. People are not ready to compromise with their freedom and individuality. Another factor which can not be denied is that they want to make their own decisions rather than accepting the decisions made by elders. They don't want their life to be dictated by others. Sometimes difference in the lifestyles between them and others in the family also forces them to make their own way. The reasons are not always unacceptable. Many people keep financially helping their main family despite living separate from it. They live away just to have a taste for new lifestyle and still remain emotionally connected with it.

Q.6 What qualities an ideal family head should have?

The head of a family must have a non-partisan attitude. He must be a good communicator and make decision in the most unbiased and neutral manner. He must keep the interests of all the concerned. The most important quality in my view is that he must run family in a democratic manner. Instead of imposing his views on all other members, he should consult all and seek their suggestions. He must have a mingling nature and must be well behaved since he is an icon for his family and his character influences all the members.

Interview 48

Part One:

1) Do you go for shopping?

Not too often. I honestly admit that I am not good at shopping. However I occasionally go for it when there is nobody who can go and buy the things for the family. I love going for window shopping with my friends.

2) Who is good at shopping in your family?

My father is a good buyer. He has a huge experience of shopping. He is good at identifying quality items and can easily decide whether to buy or not. He can hardly be conned by any merchant with his tactics and language. He can also assume the cost of any item which in most cases is almost correct.

3) What things do you enjoy buying more?

I enjoy buying my personal things like clothes and cosmetic items. I like sporting fashionable clothes and like to use branded perfumes, deodorants, skin creams, hair gel etc. That is the reason why I don't allow anybody to buy any item for me.

4) Do you like to buy from open market?

I really find it very boring because we have to move from one place to another place to buy different items. There is a question of reliability since we sometimes end up paying more than the actual price. Chances of getting duplicate items are too high. Items once sold are usually not taken back.

Part Two:

Describe a debate you participated in.
Say...
When did you participate...
What was it about...
What benefits did you get...

Ans:

I used to participate regularly in debates and discussions when I was pursuing my masters in arts. Once when I was in the first year, there was a debate organized in my college on the subject "Should children be taught in English medium schools or not..." Being the student of English literature, the subject is of an immense relevance to me. I was in the group supporting the English as a medium of instruction in formal education. I had to be extra conscious because the jury comprised of some eminent personalities of my city. The discussion went on for more than an hour. All the participants seemed to have done considerable amount of research. I too spoke on various issues related to the topic. Both the groups nicely asserted their viewpoints and refuted the arguments of their opponents. It was really a wonderful experience. Both the groups were so eloquent in their expressions and so rich in the content that the jury found it a tough task to declare the winner.

On that day, I realized how easy it is to frame a viewpoint on any issue but once we confront the opposite view, our conviction is tested and sometimes challenged and we become self suspicious. Developing a non-partisan approach to any given situation is extremely important to critically evaluate any point. I felt the importance of good communication skills. Sometimes people even having no substantial knowledge of the given subject turn the argument in their favour just because of their powerful communicating ability. I also learnt on that day how important it is to have a good oratory. Public speaking skill is not as easy as we think it to be. I here frankly admit that my group lost the debate and the opposite team was declared a winner. My friend got the special prize for his exceptional performance. Though I was the part of a losing team, I had no regret as I got to learn a lot from that experience.

Part Three:

Q.1 Why do some people feel reserved about participating in public debates?

I think the reasons vary from person to person. Public speaking is an art and all may not possess it. Most of the people are afraid to speak in public because they are not used to doing so and the fear of being wrong or being laughed at holds them back. Another main cause is that some famous people do not want to make their opinions public for the fear of being criticized if their views are deemed to be unacceptable. Sometimes people refrain from being a part of discussions on the topics which are controversial or may generate controversy.

Q.2 What should one be careful about before participating in any public discussion?

I believe that the main thing is the knowledge of that subject and one must know how to assert his views and refute others'. However, intellectual honesty is also appreciated if you acknowledge the opponent's views if they are found to be irrefutable and constructive. One should also keep in mind who the listeners are and what the debate is for. If it is a formal competition, we must vehemently express our views and strictly stick to our stand. Being a good listener is as important as being a good speaker in general public discussions. When the discussion is held to reach a consensus in on any issue or it might be a just an intellectual feast, one must be well dressed and avoid using offensive language in public discussions and debates.

Q.3 Whose public speaking skills do you admire most?

I am a great fan of Atal Bihari Bajpeyee, the former prime minister of India. He is hailed as one of the wisest and shrewdest speakers in the world. Though he speaks very slowly, his choice of words is really amazing. Journalists always find it very hard to interview him. His command on Hindi language and choice of relevant words is truly marvelous. He is a rare blending of a poet and a politician and perhaps this is the reason why he has an enviable ability to speak in public.

Q.4 Why do you think some people cannot speak well in public despite being well read and educated?

I believe that a person will prove to be a good speaker if he possesses knowledge but merely having knowledge of the subject does not make one a good speaker. Public speaking is an art and hence it needs to be cultivated. Good level of confidence and extensive practice are the two most important factors to sharpen one's speech-making. Good speakers are never born but they are made after long experience and diligence. Sometimes scholars prove to be ineffective speakers in spite of being good at language since they cannot come down to the level of listeners. The kind of words the speaker chooses should depend on who the listeners are, which is the core of a good oratory.

Q.5 Why do you think politicians are always good speakers?

It is quite understandable because they are the people who interact most with people and that too with people from different walks of life. Being politicians, they have to take stands on various issues concerning public interest and must effectively affirm them. When in power, they have to make policies and when in opposition, they have to criticize the policies made by the party in power. Moreover, they often address public gatherings and face media. All these experiences eventually make them smart and sharp speakers.

Q.6 Do you think politicians actually believe in what they speak?

Politicians, being endowed with an important task of making decisions on behalf of us, are expected to be the people of utmost integrity which unfortunately is not seen. When somebody is a member of any political party, he has to ensure that his personal ideology doesn't contradict with that of the party he represents. Sometimes politicians issue a gag order on its members. Politicians are the representatives of their respective political parties therefore their statements are understood to be the statements of the party. No politician can afford to be dragged in any controversy if his frank individual opinion happens to be popularly unacceptable. All these factors do not allow politicians to freely express their views. Ironically so called custodians of democracy cannot enjoy their democratic right of freedom of speech and expression..

Interview 49

Part One:

1) Tell me something about your house you live in.
I live in a small bungalow in very posh area of my city. It has two bedrooms and a hall with all the required furniture and facilities. We have been living in this house for last fifteen years so we all the members are emotionally attached with it.

2) Tell me what kinds of houses are found in your city.
Mostly we have the houses with no modern trends and people prefer to live in their independent bungalows. All the houses have traditional design but recently the trend is changing and people design their houses with the help of professional architects and designers. Because of constantly soaring prices of real estate, people have now turned to flats.

3) Tell me something about your dream house.
I would love to have my house constructed near any beautiful natural place like a lake or a river. It must be far from noisy and cacophonic atmosphere of city. I would keep more space open for an excellently designed garden where I can read and write in very natural surroundings. It will have all the basic facilities and it will not be congested with unnecessary things just for the show off. I believe in simplicity and want my house to be the simple one.

4) Do you want to change anything in your existing house?
I am almost satisfied with my current house but I want to redesign my studyroom because it was made by my father and I am not happy with the way all the things are placed there. Apart from this, the drawing room is too small so I want to make it a bigger one by sacrificing the open space which is lying unused.

Part Two:

Describe something which annoys you.
Say...
what it is ...
when it started annoying you...
why it annoys you...
what do you do when it annoys you...

Ans:
I usually never lose my temper however provoking a situation might be. Though I am a peace loving person, I can't stand one thing and it is when somebody is careless about punctuality and fails to reach on time. I am very punctual in my life and strongly believe that everybody should also be punctual too. People who do not value time usually end up wasting it.When I was studying in Ahmedabad, I was also learning English language. The institute where I used to go for coaching was very famous but one tutor in that institute was notorious for coming late. First two days, I kept mum but on the third day, I drew the attention of the management towards this issue and the tutor was sacked. I was really annoyed with his habit of keeping students waiting for long time. It is no

less than an insult to keep somebody waiting unless the reason is genuine. Some people have the habit of always keeping others waiting. Not only this, they are appreciated for this considering that they must be too busy. I believe that busy people are more particular about time. I think it is very difficult to develop this habit. We can hardly find few people who take this seriously. If we look into the lives of great people of the world, we will find one common trait among all of them and that is punctuality.

I really hate being kept waiting unnecessarily and if somebody does it with me knowingly or unknowingly, I straightaway express my displeasure to the person's face whether he likes or not. I know that by doing so, I might spoil the relation with the concerned person but that person will definitely understand the importance of time and will avoid repeating the same mistake in future.

Part Three:

Q.1 Do you think a person's nature helps him or her professionally?

It is a very evident fact that good natured people always have more acceptability in their professional life. It is important to know how to build and maintain relations in our professional life and people with good nature can do it well since they easily win the trust and confidence. They create good impression in the minds of all those whom they deal with. Nobody likes to continue working with those who are ill-behaved and rude in their language. Peace loving, cool and sociable people are loved everywhere and by all.

Q.2 What kinds of circumstances usually incite anger?

To be angry or not depends upon an individual's reaction to the situation. Very often, people lose their temper when something happens against their wish. Acts against humanity like rape, violence, riots etc also make us angry. Sometimes we get angry with people when they do not behave in the way they are expected to. It is actually very difficult to state which specific situations provoke us because anger is nothing but a human reaction to a concerned situation.

Q.3 Do you think good nature can be cultivated or it is something an individual is born with?

We can not deny the factor of one's personality but to a greater extent, a person's nature can be affected by the surroundings where he is brought up and educated. That is the reason why people belonging to same academic or social background usually have predictable behaviour. It is often seen that educated people behave in more sophisticated manner than the illiterate. However, if we go by the traditional wisdom, in extreme and provoking situations, people normally behave in the way their personalities make them behave. The influence of experience and education remains there till everything is good and normal.

Q.4 Do you think that a person's religious association affects his nature?

One's religious ideology and beliefs do affect one's nature and behaviour. That is the reason why people following a specific religion are found to be of the same nature to a great extent. Even their nature becomes their identity and can be predicted to behave in a certain fashion. People following Jainism are popularly believed to be peace-loving and non-violent. Buddhists and Christians are well known for their spirit of philanthropy and generosity. Hindus are the most tolerant people believing in inclusiveness.

Q.5 Do you think our behaviour is affected by the kind of food we consume?

I firmly believe that food has nothing to do with one's behaviour. Food is for the nourishment of the body while behaviour is a mental phenomenon. It is true that people eating good and nutritious food remains healthy and enthusiastic throughout their life. I am well aware of the popular belief that people eating non vegetarian, oily and extremely spicy food are usually very aggressive and short tempered. Though it might be true, I personally do not buy this argument.

Q.6 Do you think we should change our nature with age?
With the advancement in age, we always get the new roles to play and those roles require us to behave in different manners. We can not interact with the people in our old age in the same manner as we used to do in our childhood. Newer roles and responsibilities not only change us but to a larger extent, shape our nature and we too should correspondingly respond in the same fashion in order to justify the new roles.

Interview 50

Part One:

1) Which manazines and newspapers do you read? [why]

I read the most popular English newspaper i.e. Times Of India. The main aim behind reading it regularly is to improve my English as I find its language extremely elegant. Besides, news reported in Times Of India are authentic and unbiased according to me. I do not have the habit of reading magazines regularly. But sometimes I read Yog Sandesh as my father is the subscriber of it. I find the health tips in it very beneficial to all.

2) What kinds of articles are you most interested in?[Why]

I hold keen interest in reading the commentaries by famous editors on current issues. These commentaries encompass almost all the subjects. They increase my general knowledge. Reading such articles make me think critically on every topic. Such articles also give us the chance to peep into the minds of intelligent people of our society.

3) Have you ever read a newspaper or magazine in a foreign language?[when/why]
I daily read a newspaper in English. But once I read a magazine in English, there was no specific aim behind going through that magazine. As I was traveling by train, I bought a sports magazine from a station. Since I was traveling alone, that magazine offered me the best company to easily kill time during journey. I here admit that I gained a helpful information from it.

4) Do you think reading a newspaper or magazine in a foreign language is good way to learn the language?[Why/Why not?]

Certainly, it helps in improving language but again choice of newspaper or magazine does play a role as I find the language of many newspapers substandard. I personally believe that reading newspapers or magazines in foreign language will help only if a person possesses basic knowledge of that language. It will not help the novice. The main advantage is that a person comes across a range of new words in relation to various topics. It helps build one's vocabulary. Nonetheless, there are many ways to improve the language apart from reading newspaper or magazine.

Part Two:

Describe a restaurant that you enjoyed going to.
Say...
Where the restaurant was...
Why you chose this restaurant...
What type of food you ate in this restaurant and explain why you enjoyed eating in this restaurant...

Ans:
Frankly speaking, I am not used to eating at restaurants. I here would like to share my experience of having a dinner at the one of the most famous hotels of my hometown. This restaurant is located bit far from my town in the beautiful surroundings. It's little isolated from the cacophonic environment of the city. As I had not visited it before, i did not know much about it. It was the insistence of my friend to dine in that hotel only. As it was the occasion of his wedding anniversary and the treat was being offered by him, I agreed with him. To my surprise, the infrastructure and service of the restaurant was better than I expected. I thought why I hadn't visited that restaurant despite having lived in my hometown for more than 15 years. Above all, it is the quality of the food that makes any restaurant favourite among people. When I tasted the food, I was really awestruck. It was really sumptuous and hygienic. The most fascinating aspect was that it had an open kitchen where anybody can see how the food items are prepared and what ingredients are used. We ordered for Punjabi vegetables and chapattis. The soup and buttermilk offered made me the fan of the hotel. The food was being served in the traditional plates made from the bronze. There was also a facility of eating out in an open space. I really appreciate the rates which were unbelievably reasonable. We truly felt at home. It was my best eating experience in my whole life. Even I recommend others to visit that restaurant at least once.

Part Three:

Q.1 Why do you think people go to restaurants when they want to celebrate something?
Now a days restaurants offer many services apart from eating. People can avail those facilities like children's corner, cold zone, chocolate house, banquet hall etc. the main reason is that restaurants have all the event-specific things for the celebration so the host especially doesn't have to bother about the preparation and can enjoy the event well. Being involved in the preparations mars the charm of celebration. Another reason is that people get a welcome change from their hectic schedule. And well furnished restaurants are the best place to have a good and relaxing time. In the time of stiff competition in hospitality sector, restaurants offer good services in competitive rates. So people always wish to take the advantage of that. Even good hotels and restaurants approach the prospective clients with alluring packages.

Q.2 Which are more popular in your country: fast food restaurants or traditional restaurants? Why do you think that is?
Honestly speaking, fast food restaurants are gaining in popularity. The main reason is that they are the best place to have relaxing time. Fast food restaurants provide nice and westernised environment therefore they are becoming famous among youth. Change of taste is also a reason. We eat traditional food at home but in fast food restaurant, we can have a chance to taste variety

of food items. Another reason which can not be denied is the entry of global players in this ever thriving fast food industry. Big brands stand for reliability on quality. For the young people, they are the best place to spend time gossiping with friends along with gorging on the mouth-watering food items. One can get the food in competitive rates if compared with traditional restaurants.

Q.3 Some people say that food in an expensive restaurant is always better than food in a cheap restaurant-Would you agree?

I am in firm agreement with the statement. High charging restaurants offer good quality food. Since they use good and fresh ingredients, they can not afford to offer the food in lower rates. Here I don't mean to say that less charging restaurants provide poor quality food but it is very difficult to keep trust on that food especially in the time of food inflation. Perhaps this is the reason that most successful restaurants always charge more than other restaurants. One can not take chance as far as one's health is concerned. The most common argument is that it is better to pay more than to be the victim of bad food. Expensive and famous restaurants are so concerned about their brand and goodwill that the will not take any chance to get their image tarnished among the people.

Q.4 Do you think there will be a greater choice of food available in shops in the future, or will there be less choice?

Of course, there will be greater variety. As the food industry is getting global, international players in this industry will have their outlets across the world. In the time of globalisation, people also love to hold the taste for variety of foods. Even today, we find MacDonald's, Uncle Sams, U.S pizzas etc. Another reason is that people travel a lot nowadays in the time of global economy. Every person would need the food of his choice irrespective of the place he or she is traveling. This demand of the changing times is the main motivation for the people in the food industry to cater to the newly emerging needs.

Q.5 What effects has modern technology had on the way food is produced?

Because of the technology, the food production has really soared in recent times. It is possible today to grow newer breeds of crops by changing the texture of the land. Once, people simply relied on their local farmers. Today, we depend on a global web of growers, fisheries, packers, shippers, manufacturers, retailers as well as government and industry bodies. Disease resistant vaccines are given at the time of planting in order to increase the immunity of the plant. Nowadays organic farming is in huge demand for better health.

Q.6 How important is it for a country to be able to grow all the food it needs, without importing any from other countries?

No country can afford to remain dependent on others as far as the basic necessity like food is concerned. From financial point of view too, it eats a huge amount from exchequer of the concerned Government. Instead the same fund should be spent to develop innovative technologies to grow food in the home country. Politically speaking, the exporting nation can use the dependence of the importing nation to fulfil its political ambitions at a global level. No country has the right to call itself developed if it fails to grow at least 80 percentage of the food consumed by its citizens in its own land.

Interviews In Video Cd (Questions)

Interview 1

Part One:
How much do you play everyday?
Which games do you usually like to play?
Are you happy with the time you spend behind games?
Do you find playing advantageous to you?
Can you be termed to be a good player?
Which facilities do you have in your city for sports enthusiasts?
Which gamed did you play when you were a child?

Part Two:
Describer a well known writer or philosopher whose thinking you admire most.
Say.
Who he/she is...
What his/her philosophy is...
Why do you like it...

Part Three:
What qualities should be there in a good writer?
Do you think that writers do not get enough importance in society?
What are the challenges in the life of a writer?
Can you compare the life of a writer with that of a journalist and which one excites you?
What are the challenges in writing a book in a foreign language?

Interview 2

Part One:
Can you tell me your passport number?
Since when have you had your passport?
Why did you decide to own a passport?
Do you find it advantageous to have a passport?
What procedure did you go through to get your passport issued?
Do all the members of your family have passports?
Why are you appearing for IELTS examination?

Part Two:
Speak about an article you read in the newspaper.
magazine and liked very much.
Say...
When did you read it...
Why you read it...
What was it about...
Anything special you noticed...
Part Three:
What is the role of newspapers in society?
Do you think newspapers publish lot of unnecessary news?

What are the advantages and disadvantages of reading a newspaper in a foreign language?
How does the language in the newspaper differ from the language in the magazine?
Which is the better and reliable medium to remain updated with current stories? News papers or news channels?
What are the challenges in the life of the journalist nowadays?

Interview 3

Part One:
Tell me something about your house.
What facilities do you have and not have in your house?
Do you like to live in crowded area?
Do you know your neighbours?
Who do you like among them?
Are you a good neighbour?

Part Two:
Speak about an organisation you are a member of or wish to become the member of....
Say...
Which the organisation...
How you came to know about it...
What activities it does...
How does or will it help you...

Part Three:
What are the advantages of being a leader of any organisation?
What does an individual gain by being a member of an organisation?
Why do you think spiritual organisations have a lot of members?
What is the role of social organisations in your view?
Why do you think some organisations exert pressure on governments?
Why do some people avoid being a part of any organisation and contribute in their own way?

Interview 4

Part One:
Since when have you been preparing for IELTS examination?
Does it help to improve your English language?
Which module of IELTS do you find most challenging?
How much time did you spend to prepare for it?
Can you tell me about the specific strategies you adopted to enhance your performance of speaking module?
Who should take this test in your view?

Part Two:
Describe a situation where you offended a law...
Say...
When and where...
What the law was...

What was a consequence...
Was it a learning experience...

Part Three:

Which kinds of laws are usually offended?
Do you think people do not indulge in criminal activities because they are afraid of laws?
Why do you think laws often need to be changed?
Do you support capital punishment for those who commit heinous and serious crimes?
Do you there should be a fixed punishment for each type of crime?
Should the history of an accused be taken into consideration before awarding him the punishment?

Interview 5

Part One

Do you work or are you a student?
Can you tell me about your work place?
What are your job responsibilities?
Do you enjoy your current profession?
Would you like to change your profession in the future?
What do you not like about your profession?

Part Two

Describe one of your grandparents...

Say...

What his/her name is...
How was your relationship with him/her like...
What was special about him/her...
What he/she did in his/her youth...

Part Three:

Has the role of grandparents changed, in your society these days?
Do you think there are advantages in getting older?
From what age is one considered aged, in your society?
Do you think old age is a period filled with peace or with difficulties?
What meaningful activities can a retired person involve himself in?
What is the difference between spending time with the old and with the young?
What are some ways in which your community helps the old?

Speaking Bands Descriptors

	9	8	7	6
Fluency and Coherence	• Speaks fluently with only rare repetition or self correction; any hesitation is content-related rather than to find words or grammar • Speaks coherently with fully appropriate cohesive features • Develops topics fully and appropriately	• Speaks fluently with only occasional repetition or self-correction; hesitation is usually content related and only rarely to search for language. • Develops topics coherently and appropriately	• Speaks at length without noticeable effort or loss of coherence • May demonstrate language related hesitation at times, or some repetition or self correction • Uses a range of connectives and discourse markers with some flexibility	• Is willing to speak at length, though may lose coherence at times due to occasional repetition, self correction or hesitation • Uses a range of connectives and discourse markers but not always appropriately
Lexical Resource	• Uses vocabulary with full flexibility and precision in all topics • Uses idiomatic language naturally and accurately	• Uses a wide vocabulary resource readily and flexibly to convey precise meaning • Uses less common and idiomatic vocabulary skillfully with occasional inaccuracies • Uses paraphrases effectively as required	• Uses vocabulary resource flexibly to discuss a variety of topics • Uses some less common and idiomatic vocabulary and shows some awareness of style and collocation with some inappropriate choices • Uses paraphrases effectively	• Has a wide enough vocabulary to discuss topics at length and make meaning clear in spite of inappropriacies • Generally paraphrases successfully
Grammatical range and Accuracy	• Uses a full range of structures naturally and appropriately • Produces consistently accurate structures apart from slips characteristic of native speaker speech	• Uses a wide range of structures flexibility • Produces a majority of error free sentences with only very occasional in appropriacies or basic systematic errors	• Uses a range of complex structures with some flexibility • Frequently produces error free sentences though some grammatical mistakes persist	• Uses a mix of simple and complex structures but with limited flexibility • May make frequent mistakes with complex structures though these rarely cause comprehension
Pronunciation	• Uses a full range of pronunciation features with precision and subtlety • Sustains flexible use of features throughout • Is effortless to understand	• Uses a wide range of pronunciation features. • Sustains flexible use of features with only occasional lapses • Is easy to understand throughout L1 accent has minimal effect on intelligibility	• Shows all the positive features of band 6 and some but not all of the positive features of band 8	• Uses a range of pronunciation features with mixed control • Shows some effective use of features but this is not sustained • Can generally be understood throughout though mispronunciation of individual words or sounds reduces clarity at times

5	4	3	2	1
• Usually maintains flow of speech but uses repetition, self correction or slow speech to keep going • May overuse certain connectives and discourse markers • Produces simple speech fluently, but more complex communication causes fluency problems	• Cannot respond without noticeable pauses and may speak slowly with frequent repetition and self correction • Links basic sentences but with repetitious use of simple connectives and some breakdowns in coherence	• Speaks with long pauses • Has limited ability to link simple sentences • Gives only simple responses and is frequently unable to convey basic message	• Pauses lengthily before most words • Little communication possible	• No communication possible • No retable language
• Manages to talk about familiar and unfamiliar topics but uses vocabulary with limited flexibility • Attempts to use paraphrases but with mixed success	• Is able to talk about familiar topics but can only convey basic meaning on unfamiliar topics and makes frequent errors in word choice • Rarely attempts paraphrases	• Uses simple vocabulary to convey personal information • Has insufficient vocabulary for less familiar topics	• Only produces isolated words or memorized utterances	
• Produces basic sentence forms with reasonable accuracy • Uses a limited range of more complex structures but these usually contain errors and may cause some comprehension problems	• Produces basic sentence forms and some correct simple sentences but subordinate structures are rare • Errors are frequent and may lead to misunderstanding	• Attempts basic sentence forms but with limited success or relies on apparently memorized utterances • Makes numerous errors except in memorized expressions	• Cannot produce basic sentence forms	
• Shows all the positive features of band 4 and some but not all, of the positive features of band 6	• Uses a limited range of pronunciation features • Attempts to control features but lapses are frequent • Mispronunciations are frequent and cause some difficulty for the listener	• Shows some of the features of band 2 and some but not all of the positive features of band 4	• Speech is often unintelligible	

Available at...

Book shop	Phone
AHMEDABAD	
Atul Book stall	25356178
Book plaza	26440763
Crossword	26424907
New zaveri Book	25357232
Reading tree	64501308
Sagar Books	25354250
AMRITSAR	
Sunder Book depot	2544491
ANAND	
Ajay Book stall	238237
Rupal Book stall	237171
BENGALURU	
Prism Books	26714108/3979
Gangaram Book house	25581618
Sapna Book house	22266088
Crossword	25582411
Higginbothams	25325422
Educational suppliers	2676189
Book paradise	26637466
BARODA	
Book world	2361012
Bindoo agency	2438602
Crossword	2333338
Bansal Books stall	2326109
BHOPAL	
Lyall Book depot	2543624
CALICUT	
Prism Books	9447884564
Edumart	2372817
TBS publishers Dist	2720085
H & c stores	2720620
CHANDIGARH	
Shivalik Book centre	2704768
Universal Book store	2702558
Capital Book store	2702594/2260
Variety book store	2702241
Book club enterprise	9815315447
CHENNAI	
Prism Books	42867509
Higginbothams	28513519
COIMBATORE	
TBH publishers & Dist	2520491/6
Cheran Books House	2396623
ERNAKULAM(KOCHI)	
Prism Book pvt. ltd	4000945/2206011
Higginbhothams	2368834
Pai & company	2361020/025
Educational publishers	2372817
D.C.Books	2391295
H & c stores	2375649/5563
Surya Books	2365149
Current Books	2351590
KOTTAYAM	
D.C.Books	2560599
learner's Books	2567438
H & c stores	2304351
Pai & company	2562391
V publishers Book stall	2567470
Book centre	2566992
KOLKATA	
Prism books	24297957/59
LUCKNOW	
Books & Books	2281417
Universal Book Sellers	225894
LUDHIANA	
Amit Book depot	5022930
MUMBAI	
Student's agencies	40496161
Union Book stall	24223069
Sterling Book house	22612521
Universal Book corp	22078096
NADIAD	
Student Book stall	2520447
NAVSARI	
College store	258642
NEW DELHI	
GBD Books	23260022
Jain Book Agency	23416390/91
Om Book shop	24653792
General Book shop	23263695
Jain Book depot	23416101
PALAKKAD	
H & c stores	2526317
PATIALA	
Goel sons	2213643
Pepsu Book Depot	2302851
Readers paradise	2215170
PUNA	
Manneys Booksellers	26131683
Goel Book Agencies	24452176
The word Book shop	26133118
Vikas Books	24468737
RAJKOT	
Old & New Book shop	2466195
SURAT	
popular book centre	23474165
lucky book store	22476530
book point	2744231
THRISSUR	
cosmo books	2335292
Green Books	2361038/14600
H & c stores	2421462
D.c.books	2444322
HISSAR	
Krishna book depot	235678
HYDERABAD	
Universal book showroom	24757206
Prism Books	23261828
The book syndicate	23445622
INDORE	
Readers paradise	4075789
Sri indore Book depot	2432479
JALANDHAR	
Kiran book shop	2214170
Subhas Book Depot	2225081
Paramvir enterprises	2236248
Cheap Book store	2213183
Literature House	2281055
City Book shop	2211800
KOLAM	
H & c stores	2765421
KOZHIKODE	
Cosmo books	2703487
H & c stores	2720620/1791
NEPAL (KATHMANDU)	
Ekta books Distributors	4245787
National book centre	4221269
SAUDI ARABIA	
jarir book store(Riyadh)	4626000
THIRUVANTHAPURAM	
prism books	2365063
higginbothams	2331622
modern book centre	2331826
D.c books	2453379
prabhus books	2478397
Academic book House	2331878
TBS publishers Dist	2720085/6
pai & co	2453179
continental books	2461426
VALSAD	
Bulsar book depot	222377
COLOMBO(SRILANKA)	
CG Associates	4921546/4816726
sarasavi book shop	2821454
vijitha yapa book shop	2816510
jeya book centre	2438227
Expographic books	2787140/41
MALAYSIA	
Everbest media sdn.Bhd(K.l)	61842003
crescent books (K.L)	61842448